GOLD:

How To Go From Lost to Found, Awaken Your Inner Power, and Discover Your Midas Touch

Vicki Lynn King

This book is dedicated to my brother Michael who fought for his life and won.

You are never too young or too old to change your life!

You are never too young or too old to dream and to see your

dreams come true.

"Nobody can go back and start a new beginning, but anyone can start today and make a new ending."

—Maria Robinson

Copyright © 2015 Best Seller Publishing® LLC
All rights reserved. No part of this book may be used or reproduced in any manner whatsoever without prior written consent of the authors, except as provided by the United States of America copyright law.

Published by Best Seller Publishing®, Pasadena, CA
Best Seller Publishing® is a registered trademark
Printed in the United States of America.

ISBN-13: 978-1508849605
ISBN-10: 1508849609

This publication is designed to provide accurate and authoritative information with regard to the subject matter covered. It is sold with the understanding that the publisher is not engaged in rendering legal, accounting, or other professional advice. If legal advice or other expert assistance is required, the services of a competent professional should be sought. The opinions expressed by the authors in this book are not endorsed by Best Seller Publishing® and are the sole responsibility of the author rendering the opinion.

Most Best Seller Publishing® titles are available at special quantity discounts for bulk purchases for sales promotions, premiums, fundraising, and educational use. Special versions or book excerpts can also be created to fit specific needs.

For more information, please write:
Best Seller Publishing®
1346 Walnut Street, #205
Pasadena, CA 91106
or call 1(626) 765 9750
Toll Free: 1(844) 850-3500
Visit us online at: www.BestSellerPublishing.org

Contents

Introduction 6
Part 1 Beginning the Journey 8
    Chapter 1 Where I Started 9
    Chapter 2 Where I Wandered 14
    Chapter 3 Where I Headed Next 22
    Chapter 4 Rest and Relaxation 26
    Chapter 5 Worry 30
    Chapter 6 Why Gratitude 35
    Chapter 7 Looking Ahead 41
Part 2 Creating the Life You Love 45
    Chapter 8 Finding What You Love 46
    Chapter 9 Goal? What's A Goal? 57
    Chapter 10 Don't Believe Everything
                 You Think 67
    Chapter 11 Attitude and Perseverance
                 Affect Everything 74
    Chapter 12 Who Are You, and Why Would
                 You Deserve Your Dreams? 86
    Chapter 13 Co-Creating Your Life 95
    Chapter 14 Visualization 114
    Chapter 15 What If Your Dreams Are
                 Not Becoming Reality 130
    Chapter 16 It's All About Love 138
In Closing 145
About the Author 151

Introduction

As I look out my living room window, I am astounded by the sight that surrounds me—evergreen trees and deciduous tree branches covered with a cozy blanket of white frost so beautiful that I have to catch my breath. This is a sight I have rarely seen in my life. It's as if the heavens have opened up and sifted the most sparkling powdered sugar I have ever seen onto the world around me. It sweetens my day and makes me wonder how many times in my life I had *not* noticed something as beautiful as this.

Not long ago I decided to slow down my work life and move into a part-time position. I am sitting here now, rocking in my comfy glider rocker, contemplating what I will do next. Surely there must be something I should be doing. I wonder if I could just sit here. Would that be acceptable? I'm thinking I *must* have to do something productive. Maybe I could run some errands or clean the house or pay some bills. I need something to do. I mean, who would just sit around all day and do nothing? Maybe I should go to the local shopping center and get a part time job as a greeter. Here I am, closing in on sixty-three and wondering where all the time went.

Seems like just yesterday I was that wide-eyed schoolgirl who would lie in the green, green grass and look up at the clouds, dreaming of all the adventures to come. What has happened to that girl? As I write this I am looking down at the wrinkled hands of an older woman. My mom used to tell me that when she was around her adult children and we were all laughing and having a good time, she would think she was still young. Then when she went home and looked into the mirror she was shocked to see wrinkles and gray hair looking back at her. Now I know what she meant. It was like some clever thief had stolen the years from me and replaced them with more facial hair than I could keep up with.

Part 1
Beginning the Journey

"A journey of a thousand miles must begin with a single step."

—Lao Tzu

Chapter 1
Where I Started

"If you don't know where you are going, any road will get you there."

—Lewis Carroll

I was born way back in the dark ages—1950, to be exact. Back then there were no such things as personal computers. A tweet was something that came from a soon-to-be-mother robin in the early spring. If we wanted to talk to someone, we actually walked up to him, looked him in the eye, and began a stimulating conversation. We didn't "LOL" online; we actually laughed with our best friend while in her company. If we drove into the ditch in the middle of a snowstorm, we didn't whip out our cell phones and call for help. We could call for help by rolling down the window and yelling, but nobody would hear us above the howling wind in the middle of nowhere. Seriously, though, I want you to know I am not complaining about technology. I don't know what I would do without my computer, cell phone, and e-mail. I'm just saying it was a very different time back then.

Chapter 1 Where I Started

I grew up in a small town in Iowa. It was a great place to live and very safe. Most of the time we didn't even lock our doors. We grew three things in Iowa—corn, beans, and children. I loved growing up in the Heartland, even though we were often made fun of and misunderstood. Someone once told me that Iowa stood for "Idiots Out Walking Around." I just laughed, knowing that the real idiot was the one who came up with that saying. My cousins from another state once asked if we had running water and electricity. I wondered if they had ever looked at a map.

I suppose I was the average child with the average family. There was plenty of fun and plenty of heartache as well. We all learn to deal with whatever cards are dealt us. Some of us learn quickly, and some of us take a lifetime. It seems that families are similar wherever you grow up, and we were no exception. There were hard times, good times, and confusing times—all interwoven to become the fabric of our lives.

One of the joys of my life was singing. I think it was the one thing that helped me through my hard times. I was one of those kids who could naturally sing from a very young age, and everywhere we went people wanted me to sing.

When I was in sixth grade, I sang "Moon River" in a big variety show held at our junior high school's auditorium for the parents of the school children in our town of ten thousand. The auditorium was packed! When I finished my song, I left the stage and walked down the aisle to my seat. I couldn't figure out why all the people were standing up and clapping. It was a strange sight, and everyone was looking at me. It was sort of scary, so I quickly made my way outside. My mom came running out to find me and said, "Vicki, they want you to do an encore." Well, that would have been fine with me, but I didn't know what an encore was. Mom explained to me they wanted me to sing another song. I didn't have another song to sing, so I sang "Moon River" one more time. It makes me smile to think of such an innocent time in my life.

When I was fifteen years old, we moved from the small town where I grew up. We planted ourselves on a small plot of land in the country about eight miles from the nearest town. Some of us wanted to raise horses and some of us did not, but we all wanted to live in the country where

Chapter 1 Where I Started

the air was fresh and there was plenty of room to run. Mom and Dad owned a small acreage—forty acres, to be exact. It was a beautiful place filled with green grass and white fences. There were plenty of trees to climb, barns to explore, and forts to build. My brother and I transformed a corncrib into an elaborate clubhouse where we would pass the time dreaming up our next big escapade. He was five years younger than I, and we were best buds.

I used to climb the tallest tree on the place and just sit there for hours. The view from up there was so different. I was above it all, perched like a bird on the rough bark. I would leave my youthful problems behind and stare into a clear, blue sky. I felt free and could see for miles. I could almost see my future through eyes filled with anticipation. Fifteen—what a wonderful age to be!

What would I do when I grew up? I wanted to do so many things. I wanted to write books and be a singer and songwriter. I wanted to record albums and travel to see the wonders of the world. I wanted to help others. I wanted to make a difference. I wanted my life to matter. The world was wide open to me. There wasn't anything I couldn't do!

"Do not lose hold of your dreams or aspirations. For if you do, you may still exist but you have ceased to live."

—Henry David Thoreau

Chapter 2

Where I Wandered

"Variety's the very spice of life that gives it all its flavor."

—William Cowper

The variety of things I have done in my life would probably bring a chuckle to your day. I was once a very serious equestrian. Part of my work in this field included taking young horses and breaking them to ride. I would train them so their owners could show them or just ride for their own enjoyment. Even though I was not the original horse whisperer, eventually I could persuade most horses to do what I wanted. Along the way there were a few bumps and bruises. There were a few horses I had to wrestle with, and I wasn't a big, muscle-bound girl. I was only five-six and 129 pounds soaking wet. Other than being stomped on, having a horse fall on me, and running from another one that tried to kill me, it was a rewarding career. I decided to leave it behind, however, as it was hazardous to my health.

My next career move was to become a nurse, where I could avoid bumps and bruises altogether—or so I thought. Nursing was one of the few career choices open to women at the time. It took a lot of work and some serious study to get through school and pass the boards. Pass I did, and I moved on to working in a hospital as a registered nurse on the medical/surgical floor during the night shift. I was the only RN in a small hospital during the night, so I also was in charge of the emergency room and the coronary care unit on my overnight shifts. I would go to work with intense anxiety, so afraid that someone in the coronary care unit would arrest and I would have to call a code blue on my shift. I also had nightmares about someone coming into the ER with a gunshot wound, or perhaps an earthquake would strike Iowa, or a volcano would erupt. There I would be, covered in hot lava, the only nurse in charge to deal with the situation. Strangely enough, one of those things did happen, and I survived.

I continued to work as a nurse for a number of years but changed my specialty to the operating room. There I could work with a doctor by my side and *he* would be the one who held the responsibility of life or death in his hands. I would just assist him.

For my next career, I decided to take a crack at singing professionally, one of my secret longings. I had

Chapter 2 Where I Wandered

dreamed of being a singer since I was a little girl. In grade school, I often practiced signing my autograph over and over, trying to decide which signature would look the best when I became a famous singer.

My singing career was a remarkable journey. At age thirty-four, I started getting in touch with my creative side and began writing songs. Most of them were best suited for the trashcan, but a couple of them turned out fairly well. I also entered a number of singing contests to see how I would do. I entered state fair talent contests and did win some. Mixed in with the wins were also some losses.

I decided to enter a contest that was nationwide, kind of like *American Idol*. I believed if I could just win *this* contest, fortune would smile on me, and all my childhood dreams would come true. The first year in the contest, I only made it to the regional finals, but I was pretty happy with that. I then made the bold decision to continue entering the contest every year until *I* was the winner. With one hundred thousand people competing in the contest each year, this was a very lofty goal. Would I still be hobbling up to the stage with my walker and my hearing aids to compete? How long would they let a little old lady continue to sing in this contest?

GOLD

Interestingly enough, the second year in the competition I made it to the national finals! I was filled with excitement and anticipation. Would this be my big year? The prize was amazing—a lot of cash, a major recording contract, and a brand-new pickup truck! Unfortunately, I finished the contest in second place. While the winner garnered all the money and the honors, the second-place finisher got zip, zilch, *nada*.

Most of my family came to each contest, and they just *knew* I would win. When I did not (which happened on several occasions), they were very disappointed, and so was I. I seriously considered whether I could continue on in the contest, but I did decide to continue, even in the midst of the heartbreak of losing. Keep in mind that this was a childhood dream, dangling in front of me like the proverbial carrot on a stick, or in my case, the chocolate brownie covered with pecans.

For my third year's efforts I also came up empty-handed, as I lost out at the state level of the contest. Losing at state really took the wind out of my sails!

At this point I learned—*for the first time*—one of the most valuable lessons of my life. Success does not come to the most talented or the most brilliant. It doesn't

Chapter 2 Where I Wandered

come to the one who is the best looking or the one with the most money. Success is the result of wanting something *so* much that nothing can stop you from getting it. It is not failure to lose. In every adversity there is a lesson to be learned. To be a success, all you have to do is continually pick yourself up and go on until you get what you are longing for. Perseverance is the key to unlocking your dreams.

I entered my fourth year of the competition with a new attitude. My thoughts were not about comparing myself to the other contestants. That concept is pretty amazing when you think about it, since the whole point of a contest is comparing. My Creator had taught me *not* to compare, but to bring my gifts—such as they were—to Him. I was there to perform the songs I had written—songs from my heart, as only I could sing them. I just needed to be a channel for God to flow through. I would sing and He would touch the people. The finals took place on *national television*. I stood behind the enormous, sparkling curtains of the Grand Ole Opry in Nashville, Tennessee, and I *knew* it was my turn. As I heard my name announced and saw the curtains parting in front of me, I was in my *bliss*! I enjoyed that performance more than any other and connected with my audience in a mysterious and powerful way. In fact, in the *middle* of my second song, the audience spontaneously burst into applause as I was singing!

As I signed autographs for the many people who flocked to the stage just to meet me, the national champion, *I* was the one being blessed. This is a lesson I hoped I would not forget. All the hours of practicing, praying, crying, trusting, sometimes doubting, and yet still persevering, had brought me to this place. It's a wonderful thing to see a goal fulfilled—to see a dream take shape and become reality.

As amazing as it was to have reached my goal and reap the monetary rewards, other rewards were even more fulfilling. I soaked up all the encouragement offered to me from so many people! A lot of that support came during the contest years and much of it came in the following years of my singing career. There were many very kind people who connected to my songs and to me. They were always quick to brighten my day with praise and the phrase I heard everywhere I went—"keep singing."

I continued to sing in a variety of different venues and shared my music with many. I had songs released on national radio and a music video released nationally, along

Chapter 2 Where I Wandered

with TV appearances. In fact, my music video was at one time in the top twenty music videos when it was released.

It was an invigorating time in my life! God blessed me in so many ways because I trusted in Him and persisted in the quest toward my goal. I was even offered a contract to be the opening act for a *very* famous country music star on his national tour. This offer I declined, but my point is, *it was there for the taking.*

I sometimes think back to those days and the thrill of it all! I think about what I would have missed out on if I had quit the contest after that third year, when I was so disappointed in losing for the third time in a row.

I am reminded of something we did so often as children. We would be dying of thirst from the hard work of playing outside, and we needed water! Our play was much too important to take time out to go into the house and get a drink, so we would use the old pump that was in the yard. To get water from this pump you first picked up the can next to it where there was a little water saved for just such an occasion. The water was not for drinking but for priming the pump. One of us would pour that water down inside the pump, and the other one would pump like crazy. Sometimes you had to keep going up and down on that pump for a long time before your reward came. Then, suddenly, there would burst from the spout the most clear, cool, delicious water we had ever tasted. We would drink and drink of that water until our thirsts were quenched and our clothes were drenched.

I have seen in my life that all too often people stop priming the pump. You have to pump and pump even though no water is coming out, you must keep pumping. If you stop the moment before the water spurts out, you will never *taste* it, even though you were only seconds away from getting what you were looking for. You must keep pumping until you get the results you are seeking.

"Many of life's failures are people who did not realize how close they were to success when they gave up."

—Thomas Edison

Chapter 3
Where I Headed Next

"Your present circumstances don't determine where you go; they merely determine where you start."

—Nida Qubein

I was sitting at home one afternoon minding my own business when a gentleman called me on the phone and asked if he could visit with me about a brand of insurance I had never heard of. I remember thinking to myself: "Insurance ... what could be more exciting than that?"

I decided to listen to his offer, whatever it might be. He came to my house and talked with me about getting my insurance license because someone he knew had recommended me for a career in sales. I thought about it for a while and remembered that I had always wanted to be a secret agent—maybe I could be an insurance agent instead! I was still singing and doing concerts, so I thought this might be a good side business. After I heard what kind of insurance it was and how it could be so helpful to people in their everyday lives, I was impressed. I went through some insurance classes and passed the licensing exam to begin my insurance adventure. Insurance adventure: sounds like an oxymoron, doesn't it?

Actually, I enjoyed this career move very much. I worked as an associate for a few years and then was asked to move into a management position. In this position I had to recruit and build a team of secret agents to work with me on various assignments. If we decided to accept the current assignment, our message would self-destruct in thirty ... oh, excuse me, I got off the track. Reality check!

I found the job to be very challenging and very hard work, but I did enjoy building my team and helping them to become successful. I got to know my team members and shared in their good times and challenging times. I felt that we were doing important work in helping our clients financially as they dealt with difficulties in life. After seven years in that position with my team growing and doing well, I was asked to move up to become a Regional Sales Coordinator. (I was also privileged to have the opportunity to sing and open many corporate meetings for this Fortune 200 company!)

As a regional manager, one of my duties was to recruit good people for my management team to train and

Chapter 3 Where I Headed Next

work with. The team was always growing and changing. I also held meetings where we had training and motivational activities. I relished the times when I had parties for my team, meeting to celebrate and have fun together, always accompanied by good food, of course! We had a few golf tournaments, which were quite hilarious. Some people loved golfing and others—well, I will just say that we had awards such as "shortest drive" of the tournament. Most of them were really good sports, and we had some great times together.

After several years of being in this position, I realized that *twelve* years had gone by, and I felt like I had missed out on much of my life by working so hard. There is an abundance of stress in any sales management position, because the quotas are always growing and the hours for a personal life are always shrinking. At the end of every December it seemed like we celebrated for about five minutes. Then January first came, and it was time to start all over again with new, larger quotas and more deadlines. As my state sales coordinator used to say, "On January first everyone goes from hero to zero."

Don't get me wrong, I enjoyed the challenge of the job and I appreciated the company, but I felt that my time in the corporate world needed to come to an end. I was exhausted! As I was getting my taxes done that year, my CPA said to me, "Why are you doing this?" He was asking why I was choosing to step down when it would cut my income substantially. Why step down from a position when financially, all is going well? I told him that I was more interested in making more of my life, even if it meant making less money.

I was ready to make a change. In my last year of management with the company, I had inadvertently neglected to take care of myself. What I really needed was a little rest and relaxation. Besides, I also needed some time to spend with my sweet little grandsons!

"We make a living by what we get, but we make a life by what we give."

—Winston Churchill

Chapter 4

Rest and Relaxation

"Every now and then go away, have a little relaxation, for when you come back to your work your judgment will be surer."

—Leonardo da Vinci

I have two amazing sons who are married to talented and incredible wives who actually *like* me, the mother-in-law! I also have three adorable, intelligent, and very cute grandsons! Since I had recently exited the speeding train, a.k.a. the sales machine, I now had more freedom in my life and the ability to hop on a plane. I made the decision to spend more of my time flying out to Colorado to visit all of them. The great thing is, they live a short distance apart so I could visit all of them in one trip (and be treated like royalty, I might add). So, every few months I would take a trip and spend some quality time with my family.

I also thought about what else I wanted to do, now that I had more free time. I was still working with insurance, helping my clients with claims and selling new policies, but on a part-time basis.

I thought some time on the beach would be helpful, so I sat in the sand for a few days. Before hitting my sixties, I was a redhead, so I have to sit under an umbrella or the sun fries me like an egg on a hot sidewalk. I enjoy sitting by the ocean, though, because it helps me to put my life into perspective. The ocean is so vast, and I am like a grain of sand on the beach—one of many. I found myself asking if my life had any significance in this huge universe. Had I made a difference yet? Was I too old to make a difference now? All good questions, but how can one *know* if they have made a difference? And how old is too old? I once read an article that admonished us to: "Stay fit—when you are sixty years old, someone may ask you to do something really big."

I try to stay fit by exercising my body and my mind. Sometimes exercising my body is easier. These days, I seem to do things that surprise even me. Once in a while I put the milk into the cupboard and the cereal into the refrigerator. Last night, I apparently turned the light on in my bedroom as I was leaving the room. Later I went back and saw the light on. *Now who would have done that?* I

Chapter 4 Rest and Relaxation

thought to myself. I then went on a short trip looking for my mind. The trip was short, because I found my mind quickly. I am told that this is all a natural part of the aging process. I digress ...

Since I was taking all this time for me, I decided to record a new album or CD, whatever they call them these days. This was going to be a fun project, because it would be jazz style, which I had never done before. I chose songs that I sang as a youngster and songs I heard my extended family singing at our Sunday sing-a-longs.

My mind wanders back to days long past, fun times of singing together in my grandma's house. Mostly it was all the grownups and me. We would gather around the piano and sing for hours. My uncles played their guitars, and I was taught how to play along on a set of spoons. I loved those times, because I was crazy about singing and I also got a lot of praise from my aunts, uncles, grandma, and grandpa. What child doesn't like getting attention and admiration from adults? For some reason, one day my grandma sold her piano and movers came to haul it away. I never knew why she sold it—maybe she needed the money. It seemed that things were never the same after that.

One thing about life that never changes is that things are always changing!

"If we don't change, we don't grow. If we don't grow, we are not really living."

—Gail Sheehy

Chapter 5

Worry

"And which of you by being anxious can add one cubit to his span of life?"

—Matt. 6:27 (RSV)

I have a confession to make. Shortly after I stepped down from my corporate management job, I had somewhat of a meltdown. I was sitting around the house and then pacing around the house, wondering what to do. I used to get several phone calls a day from various agents on my team. Often my nights would be filled with calls or emails from managers or associates wanting my help. Suddenly and without warning the phone totally stopped ringing. It wouldn't ring for days on end. I would sometimes pick it up just to listen for the dial tone to make sure the phone was still working. Where had everyone gone? Nobody called to ask questions, nobody called to say hello, nobody called. It was an abrupt and unwelcome change. Why did this bother me so much? Maybe when people were calling me all the time I felt needed and therefore important. Who needed me now? What happened to my associates and my friends?

I began to go into a stall, like an airplane—engines blown, hurtling toward the ground with no hope of righting itself. I was lost, stumbling around in a darkness of my own making. My darkness was fear, and my only companion was worry. Thoughts that had haunted me for much of my *early* life came tumbling back into my mind. They tumbled quickly and relentlessly. They were the thoughts that told me I wasn't loved, I wasn't needed, and I had no value.

I felt like I was in a dense fog, unable to see the path ahead. I knew that I needed to change things and stop the downward spiral I was in. I had been to this place before, and no good ever came of it. Now I just needed to remember how I found my way out, the last time I was here.

I mentioned earlier that in the rush of my previous career, I had forgotten to take care of me. I also forgot *how* to take care of me. It seems that being busy and focusing on always doing more and doing well is a good detour around the real issues of life. When a person is very busy and very in demand, it's easy to feel important and to get your self-esteem from the many things you are *doing*. Unfortunately,

Chapter 5 Worry

this was the same detour I had taken much of my life; feeling good about what I could *do*, not who I was.

Singing was both good and bad for my life. It was good for me in that I loved doing it, but bad for me because I used singing as a gauge of my self-worth. I distinctly remember as a child thinking, *People think I'm such a good singer because I am so young. When I get older and I sing, I won't be special anymore.* Needing approval from the outside, from others, was a symptom of my low self-esteem. Treating the symptoms did not cure the illness that was at the root of my problem. I believed that I was not worth loving. I truly believed that I was not acceptable.

Maybe you have never felt this way, but if you have, I can share some of the things that helped me find my way back. One day I was listening to a meditation tape, and for the first time I heard something amazing. The words spoken softly through my headset made a very clear, resounding statement in my head. The message was: "You are a child of the universe and you have a *right* to be here." This was one of the most wonderful things I had ever heard! To me, the universe is God, my Creator. I don't claim to understand much about my Creator because He is beyond my meager comprehension. I do know this, though—when I heard those words, it was as if God Himself was speaking to me in that moment. I wish I could fully explain how *much* that statement has affected my life. It was like getting God's stamp of approval on me. I *felt* my Creator's love for me in that moment, and I began to believe that He loved me just as I was.

Prior to this, I had never really felt loved or accepted for who I was. This was not God's fault, or anyone else's. This was my own issue and stemmed from wrong thinking. I began to learn that day, that my *needs* to survive on earth are these: I need food, I need water, and I need oxygen to live. I do not *need* other people's approval. This was a new understanding for me and did, in fact, begin to change my life.

I went back to the things I had done earlier on in my life. I began to meditate again. Meditating is my way of connecting with God. I have quiet times with Him and listen to my inner voice. I began to listen to music that was soothing and uplifting. I began to do what I had learned before, but had forgotten about—being *thankful*.

What did I have to be thankful for? For *this* day, another day to live and breathe and be above the ground! It sure beats the alternative. Every moment is a gift from God,

Chapter 5 Worry

and there are incredible blessings to be thankful for in each moment. I found keys that day. Those keys helped me to unlock the door that had me trapped in that darkness.

"We have to choose joy and keep choosing it every day."

—Henri Nouwen

Chapter 6
Why Gratitude

"Gratitude unlocks the fullness of life. It turns what we have into enough, and more. It turns denial into acceptance, chaos to order, confusion to clarity. It can turn a meal into a feast, a house into a home, a stranger into a friend. Gratitude makes sense of our past, brings peace for today, and creates a vision for tomorrow."

—Melody Beattie

Why *not* gratitude? Does complaining and grumbling about my life help me in any way? Does thinking about how hard life is for me do me any good? Does wondering why I can't be happy make me happier?

I was headed back in the right direction. I was on the path toward a thankful heart. I could feel it inside—a change taking place that was bringing me "home." This was the place where I could feel at peace. This was where I had found my solace before … before I had gotten lost again.

Chapter 6 Why Gratitude

I will spare you all the many details of my early years. Suffice it to say that there were obstacles in my life that I had to learn to deal with. Hurdles so high I couldn't get over them without faith and hope.

All of my life, I had waffled between energetically going forward in my life and coasting along in a fog of depression. I think that somewhere deep inside of me—and maybe in all of us—there is a fear of change—a fear of growing. I would pull myself into my shell and hide from the world. I felt comfortable with the status quo. Change would only make things more difficult and would certainly be terrifying. I was used to being where I was and felt safe in my stagnant state of mind. Something inside of me wanted to sabotage my growth and keep me trapped, just rolling up and down the tracks of my life like I was riding on an enormous roller coaster. I found that I did not choose to move forward in my growth until the pain of my present state became greater than the pain of growing and changing.

Did you catch that? I did not choose to move forward until the pain of my present state became greater than the pain I would go through if I chose change and growth.

With the help of a remarkable therapist I chose to begin that journey when I was in my early thirties. Going through the emotional turmoil of my life was unbelievably difficult, but there was no going back. The only way out was straight ahead through all the pain and all the hard work I had to face. I walked for miles and miles along that path. I walked for years and years along that path. With an imaginary machete by my side, I would chop through the dense undergrowth of weeds that clung to the soil in the forest of my mind. Eventually I began to see the path more clearly and feel the sun on my skin as I traveled. As time went on, I began to feel free of many of the thoughts that had cluttered my mind and my emotions. I had worked and cried and shouted my way through, and it felt so good to be safely on the other side.

Then an interesting phenomenon occurred in my life. I was playing tennis one day, and I began to feel ill. I suddenly lacked the strength to even finish the game we were playing. I went home and found that I was bleeding profusely from my bladder. It frightened me, so I called the doctor and went in for an exam the next morning. He told me I was too young for the bleeding to be anything too serious. He said it was probably just a bladder infection and gave me a prescription for an antibiotic. I took the pills for

Chapter 6 Why Gratitude

several days and waited for the bleeding to stop. Instead of getting better, it got worse. Finally, I called another doctor and went in again. This doctor said I needed to see a specialist as soon as possible. His nurse set an appointment for me to see a urologist in a town about an hour away. When I saw the urologist, he did an exam called a cystoscopy. Afterward, he sat down with me, and I heard the words nobody ever wants to hear. He told me I had malignant tumors in my bladder and needed to have surgery right away. This was a Friday, so he scheduled the surgery for Monday.

I drove home alone in my car and cried. "Why now?" I asked God, "now that I am on a path to wholeness?" As I dealt with the situation and also met with my therapist later on, he told me that the physical cancer I had festering inside of me was now revealing itself to me because of the work I had done in excising the emotional cancer. Now *all* of the cancer would be removed! I had the surgery and then had chemotherapy. It was taxing, but also liberating because I truly knew I was leaving the cancers of my life behind me. I have never looked back—and I *believe* I will be cancer free for the rest of my life.

My path to wholeness is an ongoing process. It's just that—a path. I will never arrive; I will always be learning and processing. Years ago, I found this discouraging. I thought, *I've had counseling for years, and I should be* fixed *by now*. A friend of mine told me that life was kind of like peeling an onion. There are always new layers to be found and worked through. That resonated with me. Even at my age, I know I will continue to learn, because life is complicated. It seems like the older I get, the more clearly I see that I have so much to learn.

I believe that the most important discovery I made through all my issues was that I have a *choice* in what I think about all day long. I do not have to allow thoughts to run randomly through my mind controlling my feelings and therefore controlling my behavior.

This quote by Viktor E. Frankl, a Holocaust survivor, has had a great impact on my life: "Everything can be taken from a person but one thing: the last of human freedoms—to choose one's attitude in any given set of circumstances, to choose one's own way." If this survivor could choose his own way, then surely I could.

I am not sure I could have ever been truly thankful for the many blessings of my life, if I had not gone through

Chapter 6 Why Gratitude

the work of cleansing my heart and mind. I had to forgive others for things that had hurt me, which I did. I also needed to forgive myself for things that I had done. By the grace of God, I have been forgiven and am able also to forgive.

It is my intention for the rest of my life to keep my mind set on being thankful in all things. I know that I will sometimes forget to do it or just not feel like it. That will be okay, because I don't plan on being perfect. There is only One who has ever been perfect. I am determined, though, to set my intention in the right direction, because that will make all the difference in my attitude. When my attitude is one of thankfulness and hope, I will feel at peace regardless of the circumstances. I know that this will help me to make a difference in my world and will make it possible for me to really care for others.

"Happiness cannot be traveled to, owned, earned, worn or consumed. Happiness is the spiritual experience of living every minute with love, grace, and gratitude."

—Denis Waitley

Chapter 7
Looking Ahead

"Two roads diverged in a wood, and I—

I took the one less traveled by, and that has made all the difference."

—Robert Frost

I am sitting here now, rocking in my comfy glider rocker, and the question in my mind remains—where *do* I go from here? This is a new and unworn path that I see before me. There are no runway lights guiding me through the dark to my perfect destination. Actually, there are many paths from which to choose. How will I know which one to take? What should I do? That is the question. Maybe a better question is what do I *want* to do? I have "should" on myself far too many times in my life. I need to do something that will tickle my funny bone and satisfy my longings. I need to do something that makes the time fly and fills me with joy. What would that be?

Are you at a similar juncture in your life? Are you wondering how to move forward from where you now find

Chapter 7 Looking Ahead

yourself? You most likely are, and that is why you are reading this book.

My mom, my sister, my son, and I were once in a clothing store, shopping. My son was looking for a particular shirt, just the right one. He kept pulling out different shirts and holding them up to see what he thought of them. My mom turned to me and said, "How does he know what he likes?" We all instantly got the giggles at the absurdity of the question. Even years later, someone will bring it up, and we still have a good chuckle. However strange that question may sound, within it is a deeper question. How *does* one know what will make them happy? It's not really such a silly question when you think about it. We all want to do something great with our lives, something that will be fulfilling and bring us joy. We want to have a sense of purpose and to make a difference, but we don't always know what direction to go.

Here I was, trying to figure out what I really *wanted* to do now. I had no short-term goals left at this point. I was still working part time in insurance. My album was finished, I had done some traveling, I had rested with my toes in the sand, I had spent time with my kids and grandsons. I had read many books, I had played my guitar, watched some television, saw some movies, spent some time with friends, and I had rocked in my rocking chair. What did I want to do with the rest of my life?

I furtively took a peek at my list—the list of things I wanted to accomplish in my life. I knew there was something on that list that I'd always wanted to do, but never done. I had always wanted to write a book but had never even attempted it. Why you ask? Let me pull out my list of excuses—I'm too busy, I have other responsibilities, I'm too young, I don't know how, I'm too old, I can't get started, I have nothing to say, I can't afford it, no one would read it—the list goes on. I said to a friend once, "Do you know how old I will be by the time I learn to write a really good story?"

"Yes," she said, "the same age you will be if you don't."

As I was reading one day, it came back to me—the same lesson I had learned while competing in the singing contest. I am not here on earth to compare myself with others. My book does not have to compete with other books. My book doesn't have to be the funniest, most poignant book written. It doesn't have to be a bestseller. It just needs to be *my* story. I am here to share my story, such

Chapter 7 Looking Ahead

as it is. There is no one else who can do that. No one else can share this story, because it is uniquely mine. Whether it is good or not so good doesn't really matter. What matters is that I share it. Perhaps my story can touch someone else and make a difference in a life.

So, after thinking about and dreaming about writing a book for many years, I am actually doing it! This book is for you and this book is for me. I am enjoying this immensely, and I hope that some of my words will make you smile and others will make you think and help you to grow. Perhaps you will be able to take the first steps toward pursuing your dream. If you can draw one thing that will touch you from this book, it will have been worth all the effort. Thanks for joining me on this journey!

"Whatever you can do, or dream you can, begin it.
Boldness has genius, power, and magic in it."

—W. H. Murray

Part 2
Creating the Life You Love

"The real voyage of discovery consists not in seeking new landscapes, but in having new eyes!"

—Marcel Proust

Chapter 8

Finding What You Love

"To accomplish great things, we must not only act, but also dream; not only plan, but also believe."

—Anatole France

What about you? What do you delight in doing? What makes time fly? What makes you feel full of hope and excited about life? Do you know? Have you stopped long enough and looked deeply enough to figure it out? Have you taken time for *you*?

We are all born with inherent talents and abilities. Each one of us is unique and totally one of a kind. There is not *one* other person exactly like you!

In order to know who you are and what you can give to the world, you need time alone to understand yourself and fully discover who you are. You cannot hear your inner voice amid the noise and confusion of this world. When I say time alone, I mean time to be still, quiet, and listening. Your quiet space needs silence so that you can hear.

I have found that it's easier to remain busy with various activities than it is to be still. It seems that most of us would rather busy ourselves with the details of life than be still. Maybe it seems too difficult to look deeply into our own lives. It's easier not to, isn't it? There are so many things to be done. There's work, and taking care of the house, and children, and places to go and people to see. Life seems to go by faster than ever these days. The activities we can busy ourselves with are never-ending, and if that's how you want to live, it's perfectly okay. If, however, you want more—if you want to grow and thrive and be in your bliss, then give yourself the gift of quiet time to figure out who you are and what brings you joy.

For me to do this is a discipline. I know it is good for me and helps me to be a better person. Still, I can bypass my own good in the name of being productive and getting things done. I have to carve out a few minutes of my own each day. It's kind of like physical exercise. Not all of us make time to do it on a regular basis, but we all know it's good for us. I know exercise is good for me, but I do not enjoy doing it. On the other hand, when I take quiet

Chapter 8 Finding What You Love

time just for me, I enjoy it very much, and the benefits are always visible in my life!

So back to my first question in this chapter: What about you? What is it that makes you feel alive and fully engaged in life? What gifts are uniquely yours to share? Do you have some of them figured out? If so, start there and build on what you know.

Maybe you love to paint or draw. I would love to be able to do that, but all I get when I try to draw are stick people. Are you happy when writing or singing? Sing in the shower, out of the shower, in church, in a nursing home, in a coffee house, or for your children or grandchildren. Write your story—funny or serious, it doesn't matter; it is yours to write and yours to share with just a few or with many. Are you good at decorating? Help someone decorate his or her home. Start a small decorating business and see where it goes. Are you a seamstress or do you love knitting? Do you like to bake? Maybe you could bake some lovely pies to share, or you could sell them and have your own small business. Perhaps you enjoy reading—then by all means read and maybe read a book to someone who can't. How about *active listening*—is it a skill you have or can learn? Almost no one really listens anymore. People are *longing* for someone to listen, to pay attention, and to care. Look up "active listening" on the Internet, and learn how to make this a skill you can use to help others feel cared for.

If you are doing something that blesses you and brings you joy, you are on the right track. If you share your joy, you will bring value to the world. I don't know what you long to do, but you do! Only *you* know what your heart yearns for.

Now you might say, "I don't have the time or the money to do anything for myself." I don't know your financial situation, but mine hasn't been so great many times in my life. I have found that finances don't need to hold you back from taking a little time just for you. It is all about priorities.

I was in a counseling session, in my thirties, and I told my therapist that I could not afford to hire a babysitter to watch my children while I took time just for me. He looked me in the eye and he said, "How much are you worth? Are you worth spending a small amount of money so that you can take better care of you?" He also told me I would be a much better mother if I did take care of myself. As mothers we get caught in the trap of always taking care of others and usually forgetting to care of ourselves. You

Chapter 8 Finding What You Love

know how in an airplane they make the safety announcements? One of the funniest I've heard went like this: "In the unlikely event that our flight today becomes a cruise, please put on the yellow life vest that is stowed under your seat." Usually, though, the flight attendant gets on the microphone and says something like, "In the unlikely event of an emergency, your oxygen mask may drop down." Then they *always* tell you to secure your own mask *first* before helping others. Whenever I fly, I think about how well that statement relates to life in general. If I am depleted, I have nothing to give—to anyone. If my tank is empty, I need to fill it.

An essential practice in my life is meditating. For me, this doesn't mean sitting in a lotus position with my fingers and thumbs touching while chanting *ohm*. I know that is a wonderful way to meditate, but it's not what I use. The point is to find a meditation practice that works for you. There are so many good CDs out there with wonderful guided meditations and beautiful music in the background. I have even found some great ones in an MP3 format on the Internet that I have downloaded for *free* onto my computer. Guided meditations can help you keep your mind calm and focused. Now don't worry, this doesn't take all day to do! Actually, there are many guided meditations that take as little as five minutes. You most likely have five minutes to spend on yourself, do you not? Remember—you are worth it! It's all about priorities.

Because of our busy lives and all of the many things we have to get done each day, it is often difficult to keep focused. Just remember that it is okay for your mind to wander. When you notice that you have stopped meditating and have started thinking about something else, it is okay—just gently bring your thoughts back to the meditation and continue. This happens often, especially when you are just starting out.

One of the benefits of meditation is the deep breathing that is usually practiced. We are all in such a hurry these days and hardly ever take a deep breath. I used to think it was too much work to take a deep breath. Can you imagine that? Deep breathing is so important to good health and helping reduce the stress in our bodies.

My meditation time is all about centering myself. I connect with God, who is my source, and focus on who I *really* am. I am not my thoughts, and I am not my body. You may or may not know this, but neither are you. The essence of who you are is within you. Your body is just the vessel that your soul, your spirit, travels in throughout your

Chapter 8 Finding What You Love

life here on earth. Your body is like a container for your soul, which is the real you. It is so important to grasp this concept because it can be life changing. I have learned that my body belongs to my soul—not the other way around.

When I live as if I am just my body, my ego is always in control. My ego wants to compare me to others; my ego wants to be right; my ego wants to judge. I heard it said once that ego can stand for "*e*dging *G*od *o*ut." I want to live as authentic a life as I can, and so it is important to me to live from my center and not my circumference.

Imagine for a moment that there are no limits on your life—that whatever you want to be or do is possible for you!

Close your eyes, sit quietly, and do this brief exercise: Imagine that you now can do *anything* you want to with the rest of your life. There are no boundaries, no roadblocks in your way. See in your mind what it is that you are doing. Is there something you would love to do or be that would bring you joy? This is your imagination, and you can do anything here! See yourself on the big screen doing whatever it is that makes you *feel* excited, hopeful, alive! What if there were no limits on what you could do? Let your imagination run free. There *are* no limits on what you can imagine in your mind. Whatever you see is part of a dream in your heart.

Now pull out a piece of paper and a pen. Use it to make a dream list. Come on now; this is really fun! Stop reading, and get a pen and paper. What would you do if you could do anything? Imagine that there is nothing that is out of your reach. What do you want to do? Where do you want to go? Who do you want to meet? Imagine that the whole world is open to you. No one will see your list. Make it fabulous and make it fun! Why would you do this? To create the life that you want!

Have you ever heard of a dream board? I have made a few of them in my life and I have one currently hanging in my home. My dream board is a collection of pictures and so on that display what I desire. I cut pictures out of magazines showing places I want to go and things I want to do. I glue the pictures onto a large white board, along with some snapshots of my kids and my grandsons laughing and happy. I put pictures of myself smiling and looking happy as well. Maybe I put a word or two that has significant meaning to me. At the top of the board I write, "Thank you, God!" I keep the board up in a room where I can see it and think about it every day. This board is my private world of

Chapter 8 Finding What You Love

dreams. Here's the thing—I have had to change the board, because many of the things I have dreamed about have actually happened for me, and I needed new dreams. Also, sometimes my dreams change, and I change the board accordingly.

Are you game? I challenge you to make your own dream board and have fun with it. Remember to keep it where you will see it and think about it often.

Here's a very important truth to go along with your dream board. Whatever you focus intently upon, you will bring into your life. Now that may sound like a good thing, but it can also be negative. I will share more about this in chapter 13.

As you are thinking about your dreams, remember that there is not *one* person on this earth who is exactly like you! You have gifts that are unique to you alone. You have dreams that only you know. No one else can tell your story. No one else can create as only you can. No one else can "sing your song." No one else is a carbon copy of you. You are the only one who can leave your distinct mark on the world. No one else can give your love and your contributions to the world.

Where are your dreams? Maybe you have kept them locked up inside of you because it is safer that way. If you don't take any risks, you don't fail. If you don't long for something, you don't get hurt and disappointed when that longing is not fulfilled. One of the most ridiculous statements many of us grew up with was, "Don't get your hopes up." I say, by all means get your hopes up! Don't just get your hopes up—keep them up!

So here's the point of this whole exercise. If you don't know what it is that you want, you will (of course) not get it. If you don't have a goal to reach, you have nothing to reach *for*. The first step to finding your bliss is finding out what brings you joy.

Please take some quality time over the next few days just asking yourself, what do I really want? What is it that brings me joy and stirs up feelings of excitement? What gives me that feeling of fulfillment? What makes me feel that I am contributing to the world?

GOLD

Fill in the blanks:

Time just seems to fly by whenever I'm
_____.

Whenever I am involved in _____,
I feel so excited!

It makes me feel so good
to_____!

I wish I could do
_____every day.

When I _____, I
feel that I have really contributed to the world.

I feel like I am making a difference when I
_____.

"There are some people who live in a dream world, and there are some who face reality, and then there are those who turn one into the other."

—Douglas H Everet

Chapter 9
Goal? What's A Goal?

"A goal is a dream with a deadline."

—Napoleon Hill

We have all heard people say that we should set goals. There was a time in my life when I would run away screaming if someone would ask me to set a goal (slight exaggeration here). Seriously, though, I was dead-set against goals, and I refused to make them. I didn't think that setting goals was for me—it just wasn't necessary! I didn't have to do it, I didn't need to do it, and I didn't want to do it.

If you have no resistance to setting goals, you are truly blessed. If you *are* resistant to the whole goal-setting idea—ask yourself, *why?* That's what I had to do. As I did more thinking about my own outlook on success, I found a lot of errors in my thinking. Here are some of those thoughts about myself that I began to realize were either not true or not helpful:

Chapter 9 Goal? What's A Goal?

- I was afraid of what other people would think.
- I probably would not accomplish the goals I set.
- If I didn't accomplish those goals, I was a *failure*.
- If I didn't achieve my goals, I would be disappointed.
- If I didn't achieve my goals, others would be disappointed in

  me, especially my family.
- If I did accomplish my goals, would I be a *success*?
- If I did succeed, would others expect me to always succeed?
- If I did accomplish my goals, maybe my life would change.
- If my life changed, maybe it would change too much. Change is really scary!

I could go on, but I'm sure you get the picture. Did you see any of your thoughts in what you just read?

I was probably pretty old when I actually wrote my first goal on a piece of paper. Now you could say, "But you went to college and became a nurse—wasn't that a goal?" Yes, I did decide to do that, but it wasn't a goal I wrote down, and it wasn't what I *longed* to do. I had taken three years of private voice lessons in high school, and I started out as a music major in college. I had a music scholarship and spent a year in that college studying singing, with a desire to become a professional singer. As I said earlier, this was one of the things that I had always dreamed of doing. Sometime in that first year of college, I let the opinion of *one* person impact me. He said, "Singers are a dime a dozen—you won't be able to make it in the music business." Because I listened to this one person and let fear take hold in my life, everything changed. I decided I would quit studying music and go into nursing because I could probably be successful and happy in a nursing career. You know the rest of that story.

At age thirty-five, I began to write down my goals. While doing this for several years, I learned something valuable. Every goal did not materialize—but many of them did! This was encouraging to me, and I began to see that not *every* goal had to become a reality. The ones that did filled me with hope and joy and more faith. The ones that didn't, I either let go or kept on my goal list for the future.

This reminds me of a plaque I gave to my son Jake, who played and loved basketball. It said, "You always miss 100 percent of the shots you don't take."

Chapter 9 Goal? What's A Goal?

You will never know how important it is to write your goals down until you start to do it. If you never write down your goals, you can never even begin to reach them. As you can imagine, I learned the importance of goals big-time when I became a sales manager in the corporate world! All those many goals served me well. They brought me financial rewards and a great deal of personal growth. Without goals, I could never have succeeded in those management positions.

So what is preventing *you* from formulating some goals, and putting them on a piece of paper, or on the desktop of your computer? You don't need a long list of goals. Start with one or two goals you would really like to accomplish. These goals must be exciting to you! You must have strong feelings about these goals and what it would mean to achieve them.

I like to put my goals on paper because then I can make a copy of it and put the list in a couple of places in my house. I put them where I can see them and think about them. If you put them in a drawer you will not look at them—and seeing them every day is an important part of the process of achieving them.

Before we get more specific about goal setting, I would like to share with you some information about how your subconscious mind and your conscious mind work. The subconscious makes up about 95 percent of your mind and runs all the automatic systems of your body. It keeps you breathing, regulates your heart beating, and keeps all of your body functions working properly. It is like a huge computer that stores and retrieves data. The conscious mind makes up the other 5 percent. It is responsible for logic, reasoning, and creativity. It also controls the actions that you do intentionally. According to Dr. Bruce Lipton, a cellular biologist, the subconscious mind is one million times more powerful than the conscious mind. The subconscious mind does not think or reason—it just obeys the commands that come from the conscious mind. Think of your subconscious mind as a garden where seeds grow. The conscious mind is like a gardener who is planting seeds in that garden.

With this in mind, I would like to share with you an excerpt from Earl Nightingale's recording, which also became one of the greatest motivational books of all time, *The Strangest Secret*.

Chapter 9 Goal? What's A Goal?

Why do we become what we think about? Well, I'll tell you how it works, as far as we know. Now to do this I want to tell you about a situation that parallels the human mind. Suppose the farmer has some land, and it's good, fertile land. Now the land gives the farmer a choice. He may plant in that land whatever he chooses; the land doesn't care. It's up to the farmer to make the decision. Now remember, we're comparing the human mind with the land. Because the mind, like the land, doesn't care what you plant in it. It will return what you plant, but it doesn't care what you plant.

Now let's say that the farmer has two seeds in his hand. One is a seed of corn; the other is nightshade, a deadly poison. He digs two little holes in the earth, and he plants both seeds: one corn, the other nightshade. He covers up the holes, waters, and takes care of the land, and what will happen?

Invariably, the land will return what is planted. As is written in the Bible, "As you sow, so shall you reap." Remember, the land doesn't care. It will return poison in just as wonderful abundance as it will corn. So up come the two plants: one corn, one poison.

Now the human mind is far more fertile, far more incredible and mysterious than the land, but it works the same way. It doesn't care what we plant: success, failure, a concrete, worthwhile goal, or confusion, misunderstanding, fear, anxiety, and so on. But what we plant, it will return to us.

You see, the human mind is the last, great, unexplored continent on earth. It contains riches beyond our wildest dreams.

I will share more about how you can work with your subconscious mind to co-create your life in the next chapter. First, I wanted to give you some tips on goal setting.

1. **State your goal in a positive way using present tense.**

Here is an example of the positive: Instead of saying, "I'm going to stop spending," say, "I am so thankful that I always have enough in my checking account to pay all of my bills." Goals that are stated negatively do the exact opposite of what you want. If you are always saying to

Chapter 9 Goal? What's A Goal?

yourself "I am going to stop spending," your mind focuses on spending, not on having.

Stating your goals in present tense is important because if you are saying I want to, I plan to, or I hope to, you are actually pushing your goal into the future, rather than bringing it to fruition in the now. Another good statement in regard to your money might be, "I am so blessed to always have the money I need."

2. Write down your goal.

When you write down a goal of any kind, you activate your emotions, your intelligence, and your physical body. Writing a goal down with a pen and paper activates your visual, auditory, and kinesthetic senses. Writing the goal down on paper programs the goal into your subconscious mind, where it takes on a life of its own, working away twenty-four hours per day. (Brian Tracy)

3. Make the goal believable to yourself.

A goal that is far beyond your abilities would not be the least bit realistic or believable. Take this statement, for instance: "I have a successful and profitable craft shop. I can hardly keep enough crafts made to keep up with the demand." This for me would be a ridiculous statement because I don't like working with arts and crafts, mainly because I am not blessed with those gifts. I am not artsy nor am I crafty!

On the other hand, I knew that singing was something I excelled at, and I so delighted in connecting with the audience when I was on stage! Therefore, my goal to win a national singing contest was not unattainable. I really believed I *could* win and that made all the difference.

Belief + Perseverance = Achievement

4. **Make your goal as clear and as specific as you can.**

If your goal is to increase your income and save money, you might say something like: "My income is increasing each month, and I have $100,000 in my savings account."

5. **List all the ways that you will benefit from reaching your goal.**

If you have one or two reasons for attaining a goal, you will have a small amount of motivation. But if you have forty or fifty reasons for achieving a particular goal, you will be so motivated and determined to succeed that nothing and no one will stand in your way. (Brian Tracy)

Chapter 9 Goal? What's A Goal?

6.   Visualize your goal every day!

Take quiet time to see yourself in your imagination as having already achieved your goal. As you see yourself with your goal completed, notice how good it feels to you! The more often you do this, the sooner your goal will be realized.

"Hold an image of the life you want and that image will become fact."

—Norman Vincent Peale

Chapter 10
Don't Believe Everything You Think

"Change your thoughts and you change your world."

—Norman Vincent Peale

Wikipedia describes Murphy's Law as an adage or epigram that is typically stated as, "Anything that can go wrong will go wrong." How many people do you know who live by this law?

I hear so many people say things like this:

"Just when I think I have a little money saved up, the car breaks down or something else goes wrong, and there goes the savings."

"Yeah, I know what you mean-I fell down in the garage last night and had to go to the emergency room to get stitches. It seems like I'll never be able to get any money put away."

How about this one:

Chapter 10 Don't Believe Everything You Think

"Just my luck, I thought things were going great and then everything went to hell in a handbasket."

Have you ever heard yourself saying things like this? I know I have. Have you ever thought about the fact that when you say something, it comes out of your mouth and goes right back into your own ears? Do we really need to hear *more* negative statements? In chapter nine you read that the subconscious makes up 95 percent of our mind. It is extremely powerful and takes *literally* whatever we tell it. Then it goes to work to make that happen in our lives. Remember, it takes whatever seeds we plant and grows them.

So if you say, "Just when I think I have a little money saved up, the car breaks down or something else goes wrong, and there goes the savings," this is how your subconscious mind would handle it: *Okay, whenever there is some money in savings, something will go wrong.*

Or if you said, "I have been healthy for so long, just about the time I go on vacation I will probably get sick," your subconscious mind would say: *Okay, right before vacation I will get sick.*

Are you with me here? Before I learned this principle I would frequently say things like: "Things are so hard for me, and I am so sad. I don't think I know how to be happy." My subconscious mind would hear me and try to work out exactly what I said. *Okay, I am sad, and I don't know how to be happy.* Needless to say, I spent a lot of my time *feeling* depressed.

One day I made a conscious *decision* to change those statements. Here is what I replaced those thoughts and words with: "Everything works out great for me! I am so blessed!" Whenever I was struggling with thoughts and feelings of sadness and depression, I would stop and interject my new thoughts and words into my life. This took a ton of work and focus! It took a very long time to change this behavior, because this was changing a life-long habit. I continue to use those words today, and they have made a huge difference in my life.

Here is another statement that I chose to use when I was thinking and feeling that I did not have enough money. When caught in the grip of worry about money, I would stop and say: "I am rich, because I have exactly what I need, exactly when I need it." To me this is a profound statement. I do not *need* a bunch of stuff to make me happy.

Chapter 10 Don't Believe Everything You Think

As I mentioned earlier, my actual needs to live are these: food, water, and air. I have plenty of all of these, so I am blessed! I have much more than these—I have blessings that are far beyond just the basics, so I am doubly blessed. The statement I use the most at this point in my life is, "Thank you, God, for abundance."

Scientists tell us that 70 percent of our thoughts are negative. So we are thinking negative thoughts *most* of the time. From what I have observed in people and what I have experienced in myself, I have no doubt that this is a true statement. Why does this matter? It matters because we have what some people call ANTS, Automatic Negative Thoughts. This is a problem because if we are not watching and taking charge of our thoughts, they will *automatically* be negative. Obviously, that is not the best way to live your life.

I spoke with someone recently who told me he was often down and struggling with depression. I asked him, "When you are feeling down have you ever stopped to figure out what thoughts were going through your mind?" He said he hadn't, and I suggested to him that when he felt this way again, he could stop and list on a piece of paper the various thoughts that were running through his mind.

You might try this yourself, as I did, because it can really help to identify the thoughts that you are having. Those thoughts have a direct link to how you are feeling.

We often think that our thoughts are *who* we are. They are *not* who we are, they are just random thoughts passing through, and they do not define us unless we allow them to. I like to compare the thoughts in my head to clouds that I might observe passing by in the blue sky above. They just come and then they go. Unless we recognize and become aware of our thoughts, they can make a mess of our lives. Many of our thoughts sneak up on us from our subconscious mind.

Dr. Bruce Lipton, who I quoted earlier, says that the subconscious mind is downloading things or recording things all the time, sort of like a tape player. This begins at birth. In fact, he says that from birth to around age six, all we do is download what we are hearing and seeing (other people's words and actions) and it becomes *our* information—our words and actions. Did you catch that? You and I have downloaded information directly from our parents, siblings, peers, and teachers, to name a few. The theories and behaviors I see in others become *my* theories and behaviors. Their thoughts about life become *my*

Chapter 10 Don't Believe Everything You Think

thoughts about life. How do we know this? Brain waves can be measured by medical equipment such as an EEG machine. Scientists have proven that up until around age six theta brain waves are dominant in children. Theta brain waves are associated with a reduced state of consciousness or somnolence, almost like a hypnotic state. Therefore, from ages zero to six, children are downloading everything they see and hear.

Parents, beware, because everything you say and do is transferred directly to your young children, downloaded into their being. I'm not trying to scare you, but it's true. Believe me, none of us grew up in a perfect home. I made mistakes with my kids when they were growing up, too. I had to apologize many times. In fact, just a few weeks ago I had to tell my son that I was sorry for something I said to him—and he is thirty-four years old.

The point of this whole chapter is that your thoughts lead to your feelings, and your feelings lead to your actions. If you are thinking thoughts of doom and gloom, you will behave differently than if you are thinking thoughts of peace and joy.

Thoughts>>>>>>Feelings>>>>>>Actions

You can learn to kill the ANTS. If you want to, you can. If I can do it, anyone can! What I have found with myself and others is that change does not come easy. A person will not strive to change until the pain of being where you currently are becomes greater than the pain of working through your issues. When a person changes their thinking, without a doubt, they change their life. What do you want to think about? How do you want to feel? Where do you want to go with your life? Would you like to be able to think more uplifting thoughts? Would you like to feel happy and content? Would you like to pursue your dreams and make them come true? You can—if you choose to start with your thoughts, because that is where everything starts.

"Whatever is true, whatever is noble, whatever is right, whatever is pure, whatever is lovely, whatever is admirable—if anything is excellent or praiseworthy— *think* about such things."

—Phil. 4:8 (NIV)

Chapter 11
Attitude and Perseverance Affect Everything

"It's not what happens to you, but how you react to it that matters."

—Epictetus

This is a great quote, but do you really *believe* it, or are you like I used to be? In my younger days, I thought it wasn't true for me, because, you see, life was harder for *me* than for most people. I thought other people had it much easier than I. Nobody else had so many difficult things to deal with! When I look back on those years, I sometimes chuckle at myself. Along the way I learned that every one of us has difficulties and problems to deal with in life. That is the nature of living. It's not a contest as to who has the hardest things to deal with or a reason to stay in a "poor me" state of mind indefinitely.

Another point I want to share with you, though, is that when you do go through a difficult time, it is okay to feel *all* of your feelings. If you don't feel them, and talk about them, and work through them, they will have a detrimental effect on your life. They will be a hidden force that will impact your future and your relationships in a negative way! I am not a fan of stuffing feelings, because I have experienced the effects of that in my own life. I have seen how it can hurt not only me but also those that I love. The important thing is to identify and come to an understanding of your hurts and your issues by sharing with a family member or close friend. Granted, some people *do* have things that are more difficult to deal with. There are some very competent therapists out there who can help you deal with your hurts and problems. There are also some who aren't competent, so keep looking until you find someone who is a good fit for you.

Let me share with you a situation in my job as a district sales coordinator that really threw me for a loop. I had three part-time people put on my team in my first year as a DSC. I recruited three more people, and we had a decent year production-wise. Here is what happened in the following two years: One person moved away, two people quit, and the other three people on my team were transferred *away* from me to another DSC, who was coming into Minnesota from another state and needed some

Chapter 11 Attitude and Perseverance Affect Everything

people on his team. This left me with zero associates and a team of one: *me*. Needless to say, I was not happy about my associate moving away and not thrilled about the two who quit, but I was downright ticked off about the three people being transferred away from me! So, I thought, *what am I going to do?*

I had a decision to make. I could whine, complain, and be upset at my state manager, or I could *do* something about it. That day I *made the decision* that I would build my team by myself (with God's help, of course). I was not going to complain, and I was not going to depend on someone else to recruit people for me. I decided to continue on with a *positive* attitude and *expect* good to come to me. This was a monumental decision for me and was really a turning point in my insurance career.

After I made that decision and went to work, my team grew, and we met or exceeded our quota *every* year! By the way, the name of my team was the Dream Team. In my last year as a DSC, our team ended the year at 125 percent of our quota. Then an amazing thing happened. My state manager, who had earlier made the decision to remove those three people from my team, promoted me to regional sales coordinator. He took me out for lunch and said he would like to have me as part of his regional team. What I first had seen as an injustice to me became an opportunity to grow and expand my vision of myself *and* my team. I *know* that having those people taken away from my team was actually a blessing in disguise. God was giving me an opportunity to grow or stagnate, to open to my good or to close off my life to others and harbor resentment ... it was my choice.

One of the things I have come to learn in my life is that God is my source; people are only channels. God can use various people in our lives to bless us, but God is always the *only* source of blessings! This was an awesome realization to me because the universe (God) is always providing for me. If I lose my job, I still have income and provision, because my job is not my source, God is. My job is only one of *many* channels that my money and other blessings come through.

What I'm going to suggest may sound silly to you, but it is an illustration that really demonstrated to me the concept of God as source and people as channels. Take a piece of construction paper and poke several holes in it, then hold it up to a very bright lamp. Shut off the other lights in the room. What you see is the light shining

Chapter 11 Attitude and Perseverance Affect Everything

through several holes on that piece of paper. The lamp is the *source* of light streaming through those holes (channels) in the paper. If you tape over one or more of those holes, the light will still be shining onto the paper and will shine through the remaining holes. The holes in the paper are not what bring the light; it is the lamp that shines *through* the holes that brings the light. The universe is always there to bless you, and the universe (God) uses people as channels of the blessings that come to you. Also, when problems arise (or challenges, as I like to call them), there is always a window of opportunity for you. You can choose to see the problem as something to be angry about and a story you can tell and retell to others—thus continuing your sad story forever—or you can make a different choice and ask yourself the question, "How could I learn and grow from this painful issue before me?"

So, continuing on with my story, at the end of my first year as a regional sales coordinator (RSC) our team was number nine in the state in percent of quota. Since there were only nine regions, we had a lot of work to do. We kept working, encouraging each other, and *expecting* our team to grow and prosper. We could see that we were growing and producing more each year. After a few years of building, we reached the number one spot in the state for percent of quota! Because of the hard work of everyone on the team and our expectations of success, we were well rewarded. As an added bonus, my state manager presented me with the coveted "Manager of the Year" award.

What I learned from this particular experience is that we have choices about the way we live our lives. As you come up against challenges in your life—someone hurts you, yells at you, insults you, does something that feels unfair to you—you have a moment, probably a very brief moment (possibly even a split-second at first) to decide and choose your course of action. Here's a tip: When something like this happens you can choose to become *curious.* You can notice how you feel and ask, "Can I learn something from this?" I have found that *practicing* this approach will lengthen that split-second and give you more and more time to make a conscious choice instead of just *reacting.* I had to learn how to do this, as it does not come naturally to me. What comes naturally is to get upset, feel angry, and be offended. Getting curious as to what you can learn from the problem is a great strategy to use and can help you in making choices that are good for *you,* choices that can help you to move ahead in your growth and in your life.

Chapter 11 Attitude and Perseverance Affect Everything

Another strategy that I have found useful is to focus on *this* moment. As human beings we spend much of our time either thinking about the past and how bad it was, or thinking about the future and worrying about so many things! I like to refer to focusing on the moment as being *mindful*. When you are mindful, you are staying *present* in this moment. You are not focusing on your past and all the things that went wrong, and you are not filled with anxiety over the future. This moment is actually all you ever have. The past is only a memory, and the future has not yet arrived.

You can't go forward when you are looking back, just like you can't drive a car by looking in the rearview mirror. If you are always looking at the past, you drag the past with you into the present and live it all over again. In other words, you create a future that is just the past repeated over and over again! I know from experience that this is a destructive way to live. I also know that when I choose to be mindful, my life changes for the better—dramatically.

Did you know that you talk to yourself more than anyone else? When you are facing a challenging situation, the words you say to yourself will affect how long you will remain in the situation. Don't use your words to *describe* your situation, use your words to *change* it. One of the words that is most harmful for us to say to ourselves is *should*. When we say, I should exercise, or I should save my money, or I should be a better mom, or I should lose some weight, what happens is that it makes us feel ashamed, implies that we aren't okay, and points to our failures. If you can stop saying *should* to yourself and replace it with the word *choose,* it would be such a benefit to you. Does this sound more positive and affirming to you? I choose to exercise, I choose to save more money, I choose to spend more time with my children, I choose to lose some weight. To me it sounds more affirming and is a much more encouraging way to speak to ourselves.

We have all heard of the placebo effect. It has been proven through many clinical studies that positive thoughts bring healing on a physical level as well as an emotional level. When patients believed they were getting a new medicine to help them, they actually healed, even though the medicine they received was just a fake. Can positive thinking really change our lives? In general, I believe the answer is yes. It certainly cannot hurt us. What is the harm in learning to use positive thoughts and words in our lives?

Chapter 11 Attitude and Perseverance Affect Everything

I believe it is a much better alternative to being negative and always looking at the gloom and doom side of things.

What is your world like? Are you a glass half-empty sort of person, or do you choose to see the good in things? The most important thing to remember is that your attitude is your *choice*. The experiences we have are not nearly as important as how we *decide* to think about them. Whatever you focus on will expand in your life, so if you are focusing on all the things that are going wrong and how terrible it all is, you will have more of the same in your life! If you can learn how to focus on good coming into your life, and if you focus on being open and receptive to it, you will begin to manifest abundance in your life.

You might say to me, "That's easy for you to say." Actually, it hasn't been easy for me to say or do for much of my life. It has taken years of learning and practicing the principles I am sharing with you. Changing my attitude has made such a difference in my life. It takes a huge commitment to decide and choose a positive attitude, because you don't just choose once—you are choosing all of the time. This takes a lot of practice, but it is well worth the efforts!

Something else to consider about our attitude is another component of success: perseverance. This is the idea that we are going to persist and push on toward our goals, regardless of the results. When you have a goal and you stumble, or come up against something that seems insurmountable, it is the ability to persevere that brings success. Did you know that Thomas Edison, who was the creator of over one thousand inventions, was someone who kept a positive attitude and persevered? It took Edison literally ten thousand tries before he was able to perfect the incandescent light bulb. The interesting thing is that he didn't see his tries as failures; he looked at them in a positive way. With each attempt, he gained information on what *did not* work. This, he reasoned, brought him one step closer to a solution. He also did not doubt that he would find the right materials. When Edison reached his late sixties, the lab that he built and dearly loved caught fire and burned to the ground. This would have destroyed many people—but not Edison. "I am sixty-seven," he said after the tragedy, "but not too old to make a fresh start. I've been through a lot of things like this." He rebuilt his lab and continued to work for another seventeen years.

Anything truly worthwhile takes perseverance. We all have setbacks because things don't always go the way

Chapter 11 Attitude and Perseverance Affect Everything

we expect them to go. When we stumble or fall, what is important is to be able to get back up and go on. Facing hardships, adversity, stumbling, and falling are part of life—it is not failure! Failure is getting knocked down and *staying down*, giving up. Success is always getting up and going on with the mindset, what can I learn from this?

As we continue on to the following chapters, I will share with you several more examples from my own life—times when it became necessary for me to persevere and hold onto an attitude of hope for the future. We all come up against opposition in our lives, especially when we are pursuing our dreams. We can learn to view obstacles as challenges and opportunities to grow—not as reasons to quit! Instead of quitting, your obstacles can have the exact opposite effect. Use them to make you even more determined to succeed and to prove that you can realize your dreams. What is needed is the ability to keep that positive attitude through it all. This does not come without effort on our part. This takes practice. If you are going to do anything well, you must first *practice* to perfect the skill you are using and striving to develop. You do not learn to play the piano by taking a single lesson. You do not learn to paint by stroking the brush across one canvas. You do not learn to run a successful business by putting in one hard week. You do not learn how to bake a beautiful and delicious pie by trying only once. You do not learn how to write a book by writing one sentence. And you do not learn how to do anything well by giving it your least amount of effort.

So what I am saying is, for you to develop into a person with a sustained positive attitude and the will to persevere through any adversity will take *hard work* on your part. Will it be worth it? As one of my friends would say, "ab-so-freakin-lutely!"

"The difference in winning and losing is most often, not quitting."

—Walt Disney

Chapter 12
Who Are You, and Why Would You Deserve Your Dreams?

"See how great a love the Father has bestowed on us, that we would be called children of God; and such we are."

—1 John 3:1 (NAS)

Here is what I know: God is not an old man with a white beard and robe, sitting on a large chair in the sky. The God of the universe is the one and only, omnipotent, omnipresent, omniscient power that is everywhere around us and resides within us. God is so far beyond human understanding that no human being on this earth will *ever* comprehend Him or the power that He is.

I love this quote by James M. Boice:

There are many names for God because God is so great he cannot adequately be described by one name or even a dozen names. In fact, even the names we have do not exhaust him. They exhaust us—we will be able to spend an eternity learning of their full implications—but they do not exhaust the Inexhaustible.

As I said earlier, I often call God "The Universe." You may say God and I may say "The Universe," but in fact, we are talking about the same thing. We are talking about our source, the divine, or spirit. Keep in mind this is all about semantics and our own *personal perceptions*. What you and I call God is of no consequence to God, because He is who He is. We are just speaking in different terms, through our own filters of awareness. I use the pronouns *he* and *him* because those are words most of us are accustomed to hearing when referring to God. The pronouns are not meant to imply that I think God is a man. Jesus was a man, of that there is no doubt, because he walked upon this earth and during the years of his ministry was seen as a great teacher by many people. His words, many aspects of His life, His death, and His teachings have been recorded for us in historical books such as the Bible. He is still considered a great teacher today. Many people also consider him to be the Savior of the entire world. I believe this as well.

Chapter 12
Who Are You, and Why Would You Deserve Your Dreams?

So, who are *you* in relation to God? The verse 1 John 3:1 states that you are his child. Does this mean anything to you? If not, could it *possibly* mean something to you? Have you given it much thought?

You are a beloved child of God, and you have a right to be here. I want to share with you an excerpt from a wonderful little book that has had such a great impact on my life. Here are some words from *The Greatest Miracle in the World* by Og Mandino.

> You are the greatest miracle in the world. Those were the first words you ever heard. Then you cried. They all cry ...
>
> You arrived, bringing with you, as does every child, the message that I was not yet discouraged of man. Two cells now united in a miracle. Two cells, each containing twenty-three chromosomes and within each chromosome hundreds of genes, which would govern every characteristic about you, from the color of your eyes to the charm of your manner, to the size of your brain ... who did I bring forth? You! One of a kind. Rarest of the rare. A priceless treasure, possessed of qualities in mind and speech

and movement and appearance and actions as no other who has ever lived, lives, or shall live.

Why have you valued yourself in pennies when you are worth a king's ransom?

My pride in you knew no bounds. You were my ultimate creation, my greatest miracle. A complete living being. One who can adjust to any climate, any hardship, any challenge. One who can manage his own destiny without any interference from Me. One who can translate a sensation or perception, not by instinct, but by thought and deliberation into whatever action is best for himself and all humanity ... I gave you the power to choose ... use wisely, your power of choice ... You are more than a human being, you are a human becoming. You are capable of great wonders. Your potential is unlimited ... Wipe away your tears. Reach out, grasp my hand, and stand straight ... No longer hide your rarity in the dark. Bring it forth. Show the world ... imitate no one. Be yourself ... This day you have been notified. YOU ARE THE GREATEST MIRACLE IN THE WORLD.

Chapter 12
Who Are You, and Why Would You Deserve Your Dreams?

We all have the same birthright. Each one of us is a unique child of God. We are, each of us, loved just as we are. God does not love anyone more than He loves you. He loves each of us in the messy parts of our lives and in our successes. He loves us in the good, the bad, and the ugly parts of our personality. He *knows* our weaknesses and He loves us anyway! You do not have to change one thing about yourself for God to love you. God *is* love, and He longs for you to know that He loves you.

One of the reasons Jesus was born and lived among us over two thousand years ago was to teach us how to live. Those of us who consider ourselves Christians are known as followers of Christ. Not to put Christians down—because I am one of them—but it seems to me that we only follow him part of the time. There are some of his teachings that we sort of skip over. Let me share a few with you.

"I came that they may have life and have it abundantly" (John 10:10 NAS)

"For truly I say to you, if you have faith the size of a mustard seed, you will say to this mountain, 'Move from here to there,' and it will move; and nothing will be impossible to you" (Matt.17:20 NAS).

"My grace is sufficient for you for power is perfected in weakness" (2 Cor. 12:9 NAS).

"All things are possible to him who believes" (Mark 9:23 NAS).

"Truly, truly, I say to you, he who believes in Me, the works that I do, he will do also; and greater works than these he will do" (John 14:12 NAS).

"Come, you who are blessed of My Father, inherit the kingdom prepared for you from the foundation of the world" (Matt. 25:34 NAS).

"If you abide in Me and My words abide in you, ask whatever you wish, and it will be done for you" (John 15:7 NAS).

"Therefore I tell you, whatever you ask in prayer, believe that you have received it, and it will be yours" (Mark 11:24 ESV).

How about these verses?

Suppose one of you has a friend, and goes to him at midnight and says to him, "Friend, lend me three loaves; for a friend of mine has come to me from a journey, and I have nothing to set before him"; and

Chapter 12
Who Are You, and Why Would You Deserve Your Dreams?

from inside he answers and says, "Do not bother me; the door has already been shut and my children and I are in bed; I cannot get up and give you anything." I tell you, even though he will not get up and give him anything because he is his friend, yet because of his persistence he will get up and give him as much as he needs. So I say to you, ask, and it will be given to you; seek, and you will find; knock, and it will be opened to you. For everyone who asks, receives; and he who seeks, finds; and to him who knocks, it will be opened. (Luke 11:5–10 NAS)

It is clear to me that Jesus *never* said, "What I am doing, you will never be able to do because I am Jesus and you are just humans." No! He said, "He who believes in Me, the works that I do, he will do also" (John 14:12 NAS).

I am certainly not a biblical scholar and I have no masters or doctorate in religion. I have read, though, that the language most likely spoken by Jesus was Aramaic. I am told that the word "ask" in Aramaic could be translated as "claim." Could it be that we can claim our birthright from God? If so, why aren't we doing it? Why do we sort of skip over these particular teachings of Jesus?

It seems to me that Jesus was *repeatedly* trying to tell us that our faith, our thoughts, our beliefs, and even our persistence are very important aspects in the creation of the *circumstances* of our lives. He really wanted his disciples and all who heard His teachings to understand the principles He was teaching! That is why he continued to say the same things over and over again. He wanted these teachings to be passed down from generation to generation because His teachings are a crucial part of our universe! How did we miss it?

Clearly, some would argue that God just decides what happens in our lives. Others would say that God will only give us what is best for us in all circumstances, and sometimes our prayers are not answered the way we want because He knows best. It *is* true that God knows the big picture and we cannot see the past, present and future the way He can. So, yes, the *big picture* is far bigger than we can comprehend. It is also true that God gave us the power to choose. All of our choices deeply impact our lives, as they shape everything. Where do our choices come from? Our thoughts govern our feelings, and our feelings lead to choices. There is a rhyme and reason to our universe; we are not helpless puppets that are being moved about here and there by a God who is amusing himself. God (the

Chapter 12
Who Are You, and Why Would You Deserve Your Dreams?

universe) has given us *free will.* He will not force us to do anything. There *is* a bigger picture, if only we can have our eyes opened to *see* and grasp that there is much more going on here than is visible to us. There *is* a bigger picture; whether we perceive it or not, it is *still there*. If I should die today, that is not the end of my story. My soul, the real me, will continue on, even though my body is no longer viable.

But what if I *live?* What part do I play in creating my own life?

"Christian hope ... is not reserved merely for some splendid future yet to come. It is much more than ... a promise of heavenly reward after death. Jesus does not ask us to wait until later, until the end for help and healing. Hope is the good news of transforming grace now. We are freed not only from the fear of death but from the fear of life; we are freed for a new life, a life that is trusting, hopeful and compassionate."

—Brennan Manning

Chapter 13

Co-Creating Your Life

"With God, every day matters, every person counts. And that includes you."

—Max Lucado

Right now you may be thinking. She is so full of it! I did not have any part in creating these crappy circumstances that I am in! I didn't choose to be in debt. I don't like being overweight. I can't help it that I lost my job. It's not my fault that I don't have any friends. It's not my choice to have cancer. It's not my fault that things don't ever work out for me. It's not my fault that other people hurt my feelings. I don't choose to be unhappy. It's not my fault that life is not turning out the way I had hoped.

You know what? It's *not* your fault. You don't deserve to be blamed and shamed—not by others and not by *yourself.* You didn't *know* that this was how the universe worked! No one ever told you that you could create a better life. They said *not* to get your hopes up. They said to be practical and accept your limitations. They

Chapter 13 Co-Creating Your Life

said to be careful and avoid taking risks, because you might fail and you could get hurt. Most of us have had many of these statements said to us. How were we to know that we could actually create the life we love?

There are many things in this world that we cannot see or sense. We live on a planet that is rotating on its axis at a speed of just over one thousand miles per hour and revolving around the sun at around sixty-seven thousand miles per hour—yet we can't *feel* this happening. In addition to the fact that we can't feel the earth rotating rapidly, why do we not fly off as it rotates? We all know the answer to this: because of gravity. Can you see gravity? Certainly not, but still, we know it is there. If you throw a ball up, it will always come down because of gravity. The power of electricity has always been available on earth, but it wasn't until the 1800s that electricity became an important part of our world because it was finally discovered and understood. What about your cell phone—can you see the energy waves that flow into and out of it? My brother has a ham radio, and he told me recently that he has talked to people as far away as six thousand miles. Those radio waves cannot be seen by the naked eye, but they are present and making communication possible.

My point is that there are many things in this world that cannot be experienced with our five senses. That does not mean that they don't exist. There are laws that govern our universe. These laws are the science of the universe, laws that were established by our Creator. Just like the law of gravity or the law of mathematics, there are more laws that we can work with to create our lives. One is the law of attraction and the other is the law of vibration. When you understand these laws and are able to work *with* them you can benefit your own life and also the lives of others.

Here is what the first law states: "like attracts like." Let me explain what this means to *us*. Now, just stay with me here, because it is a little difficult to explain, but I will do my best. Everything in the world is made of energy including you, me, tables, chairs ... everything. If you took chemistry or physics in high school or college you learned about the atom, protons, neutrons, and how everything breaks down to these subatomic particles that are constantly in motion. These are invisible to the naked eye. Physicists have finally agreed that energy and matter are one and the same, which means that everything is made of energy. Energy is actually a vibration, so everything that exists vibrates. Because everything that exists vibrates, we as humans also vibrate.

Chapter 13 Co-Creating Your Life

Here is where the second law I named comes in—the law of vibration. This law is the *foundation* for the law of attraction. What is attracted to us through the law of attraction depends on the *frequency of our vibration*. There is a magnetic energy attached to our thoughts, and our thoughts are propelled through our emotions. Because the vibrational waves or emotions that we send out are magnetically charged, we are literally walking magnets, constantly pulling back into our world anything that happens to be playing at the same frequency or wavelength. For instance, when we are feeling up, filled with joy and gratitude, our emotions are sending out high-frequency vibrations that will magnetize only good "stuff" back to us. This means anything with the same high vibratory frequency that matches what we are sending out; in other words, like attracts like. If you ding a tuning fork in a room filled with many different kinds of tuning forks calibrated to various pitches, only the ones calibrated to the same frequency as the one you dinged will ding too, even if they are far from each other in a very large room. Like forces attract—this is a rule of physics.

Have you ever noticed that when you are out in public and you are feeling *really* great, it affects your experiences with other people? You are out there smiling and feeling open and vibrant, and suddenly, other people, total strangers, will notice you and smile at you, and sometimes they will just start talking to you! On the other hand, when we are experiencing anything that joy is *not*, such as fear, worry, guilt, shame, or anger, those emotions are sending out low-frequency vibrations. Since low frequencies are every bit as magnetic as high frequencies, they are going to attract only cruddy "stuff" back to us, meaning anything of that same low frequency will be returned right back to us. Whether it is high vibrational joy, or low vibrational worry, what we are putting out there in any moment is what we are attracting back to us. We are the *initiators* of our vibrations, therefore the magnets, or the cause.

Like it or not, we are co-creators of our lives. Our bodies may be flesh and blood, but first and foremost we are energy—magnetic energy. Remember too, that your body is only the container for the *real* you—your soul, your spirit. You have a brain, and your brain is the physical part of your "container," but your mind is part of your soul and as such is your connection to the mind of God.

You don't need to take my word for all of this. It has been proven by many scientific experiments that our

Chapter 13 Co-Creating Your Life

thoughts, feelings, and our DNA have a direct effect on the energy that our world is made of. If you would like to look into these experiments, I would recommend reading *The Divine Matrix* by Gregg Braden. You might also want to read *The Biology of Belief* by Bruce Lipton.

I believe we are communicating with God with every thought that we have. It might be helpful to see every thought as a "prayer" to God. The Bible says, "For your Father knows what you need, before you ask him" (Matt. 6:8 NAS). To me this means that our thoughts cry out to God and our feelings as well. Every thought brings change. Every single thought has an impact on the universe, so every thought could be seen as a "prayer."

The reason we often don't get our dreams fulfilled, our wishes realized, is because our thoughts are scattered everywhere. Instead of being like that tuning fork—laser focused on the tuning fork of the same vibration—our thoughts are more like popcorn in a popper, flying here, there, and everywhere randomly. On one hand, we pray for everything to work out, but at the same time, we worry that it won't. When we put out a positive intention and think of positive outcomes, we might *really* think that optimism is actually a waste of time.

So most of us are sending out conflicting thoughts or prayers to the universe much of the time. I pray for this; *no, that's unrealistic.* I pray for her to be healed; *but I really doubt that it will happen.* I would love to give more money to feed hungry children; *but where could that money possibly come from?* I really want to write a book; *but why would anybody want to read a book that I wrote?* The thoughts fly, the prayers go out. Scientists say that every person has thousands of thoughts per day.

It isn't that the universe (God) is not listening or answering. It's just that we are flinging thousands of thoughts (prayers) out there, and many of them are in conflict with each other. It sets up a field of intentions that are fighting against each other. Can you see how this is a problem? Opposing thoughts are setting up push/pull situations! Even God can't answer a prayer if it is in conflict with itself!

Have you ever had a difficult start to your day? Has there been a time or two that just seemed to start out bad and then went from bad to worse? How did you react? Do you think that your reaction would make a difference in how your day went?

Chapter 13 Co-Creating Your Life

Let me illustrate with Joe, for example. Joe woke up late one morning because the alarm clock did not go off. He said something like: "Oh crap!" Then on the way to the bathroom he stubbed his toe. He was in such a rush that he was short with everyone, burned his toast, couldn't find the car keys, and when he did, the car wouldn't start! He finally got the car going, and then, on the way to work, someone in another car cut him off, and he not so politely "waved" at them. When he got to work, he was late for an important meeting, and the boss reamed him out in front of his co-workers!

I am sure that you have had some experiences a little bit similar to this. There are days that just seem to start off better than others. However, as you read earlier in this book, it's not what happens to us that matters—it is how we *react* to what happens to us that matters. How we react is *everything*! As you have seen in this example, one low vibration just seemed to lead to another and then another, in a downward spiral.

I like to visualize a boomerang when I'm thinking about this principle, because it gives me a good picture of the process. You know how a boomerang works, you throw it out and it comes back to you. You either catch it or it clobbers you. That's what this process is like. What we send out is what we will get back. Focus on what we want with passion and excitement, and it's on its way to us. Focus on what we *don't* want with the same passion (such as worry, concern, fear, etc.) and *presto*, it too will be on its way.

Now, I have done my fair share of messing up my life in the past, but when I discovered these principles and found a strategy that could change my life and my circumstances, I jumped on it! As I experimented with this new system, I found that I did indeed have many successes with bringing good and positive results into my life, and it has improved with practice.

Four years before I started singing in the national contest, I went to Nashville with a friend. We decided to go to the Grand Ole Opry, but we weren't going in the front door, we were going to go backstage. We just headed into the side entrance, walking along with some other musicians and singers. We strolled into the building like we belonged there. We marched right onto the left side of the stage and watched as someone sang on center stage. People in the audience could not see us, but as I stood there, I began to think about how *wonderful* I would feel singing on that

Chapter 13 Co-Creating Your Life

stage. Before I let my negative thoughts take over, I said confidently out loud to my friend, "Someday I'm going to sing on this stage," and then I let it go. I did not try to figure out how that might or might not come about. I was just learning this new strategy back then. When I started competing in the national contest, the finals were not even held at the Grand Ole Opry, they were on a national television show. But since it took me four years to win the contest, by the time I won, the finals were held on that *same* stage, and *there I was*, experiencing what I had spoken and prayed into existence. Also, when you think about it, over the four years I competed in that contest, I competed with 100,000 people every year, so I actually had competed with 400,000 people by the time I won the finals. What are the odds of winning a contest so large? I'm not a mathematician, but I guess they are one in four hundred thousand! That result was truly something that God (the universe) and I co-created. This was *not* a coincidence.

When I spoke the words, "Someday I'm going to sing on this stage," I actually believed it in that moment. I was *certain*! A more realistic response to that statement would have been: "Yeah, like that could happen, how in the world would I ever get asked to sing on this stage?" That's what I would have thought before I learned about how my energy vibrations attract like energy to me.

Here is another example of how this works. I drove to Sioux Falls, South Dakota, a few years ago to meet my son, his wife, and my grandkids at a motel where they were briefly staying. I was going because my son had asked me if I would watch the kids for several hours, as he and his wife had some important business to attend to. I said sure, and so I was on my way to Sioux Falls early that morning in a very dense fog. The situation was quite dangerous. (If you have driven in fog, you know what I'm talking about). I felt a little afraid, as it was a two-hour drive and I didn't want to be late, but I didn't want to get into an accident either.

I drove for a while kind of nervous and worried, and then I made a different choice. I decided to make my energy vibrations positive and thank God for a safe trip. I kept saying out loud, "Thank you, thank you. I know that you will lead me safely through this fog. I know you are protecting me and guiding me all the way there." I kept saying this and kept trying to follow the lights of cars that were ahead of me. It was a four-lane road, so that helped a

Chapter 13 Co-Creating Your Life

little, but each time a car passed, the taillights quickly faded away into the fog and I could not see them to guide me.

After probably ten or fifteen minutes of saying, "Thank you, thank you for guiding me safely through this fog," a huge semi-tractor/trailer passed me. The back of it was lit up with a ton of red lights, and also on the back of the truck printed in big bold letters were the words, *Follow Me!* I started giggling and smiling and stepped on the gas. I made it safely through that fog and got to the motel on time! Coincidence? Not a chance!

Let's say that you want a different and newer car, as your car has too many miles on it. If you focus on the car you want, and keep focusing and believing that you will get it, you are more likely to get it. If, however, you focus on the fact that it hasn't come yet, or your lack of it, or how you can't afford it, then that's exactly what you'll attract: a lot more "no car."

How do I know this to be true? Not only have I experienced it many times in my life, but I have also done thirty years of study on the subject. I have read about it and talked with others who have experienced it to be true also. You might be thinking, "That doesn't make any sense; I've been focusing for years on what I want, namely more money, and I still don't have it." Right! Because first there is the subject of money, and then there is the subject of the *lack* of money. What have many of us been focusing on in our lives? We have focused on the fact that we *don't have enough money*. Focus on the *lack* of what we want and we are guaranteed to get more lack. The law of physics never changes—we get what we focus on!

Yearning for, wishing for, longing for, even hoping for are not activities of focusing on what we want, they are just negative thoughts that vibrate from a place of discouragement, a place of lack. These are thoughts born from the pessimistic belief that we will probably never have what we want. With those thoughts and accompanying feelings flowing out of us, we won't. One of the keys to this law is to focus on *already having* something you want, with *passion and joy*!

How do we do that? I like comparing it to going online to Amazon, eBay, or some other Internet store. When you order something, you don't *hope* it will come, you *know* it will come because you ordered it. Not to stereotype, but if you are a woman and you ordered, say, beautiful new curtains for your living room, you would probably look up at the old curtains and imagine those new

Chapter 13 Co-Creating Your Life

curtains hanging there, and you would smile because you know how great they are going to look in your living room when they get here! You feel happy and have a sense of anticipation.

For the guys, if you went online to the Home Depot and ordered a brand new chain saw, you might imagine how it's going to look in your hands and how it's going to roar to life when you pull that cord to start it up, and you might sound just like Tim Taylor grunting on the classic TV show *Home Improvement*.

For my musician friends, you might go to the online Guitar Center and order a new Taylor acoustic guitar. While you are waiting for it to arrive, you imagine how that guitar is going to sound when you are holding it and making it sing. You will feel excited about it coming! Again, my point is—you *know* that what you ordered is coming, and you are *certain* that it will arrive because you went online and ordered it. This is the kind of certainty it takes to put this law into effect.

Another way to state this law is that *thoughts become things.*

What does this mean? Well, think about it. Every great invention that has benefited mankind has first been a thought in the mind of the one or ones who invented it. The Wright brothers believed that a man could fly, even though others thought it was foolishness. They chose to continue thinking about how it might be accomplished and created from those thoughts the first aircraft that actually flew for a few brief moments. Henry Ford thought about creating a means of transportation other than horses. His thinking brought about his invention of the automobile. Alexander Graham Bell started to think about how we could communicate across distances, and in 1876 invented the telephone. Everything begins with a thought. Every thought is an energy wave and all things are made up of energy. The thoughts you think are always creating your world. When you have thoughts about anything you are sending out into your world either positive thoughts with the accompanying positive feelings *or* negative thoughts with the accompanying negative feelings.

Think about this, because that "coin" has two sides. The kicker here is: You cannot *not* create! You are always creating, whether you like it or not. Does that give you pause? It sure did me, and it still does every day, as I am going through all the moments of my day. I practice

Chapter 13 Co-Creating Your Life

remembering this law and try to keep my thoughts and feelings in as high a vibration as I can. It takes a lot of practice, just like becoming successful at anything does.

Sounds like a lot of work, you might say. It is work, but such amazing and gratifying work! The work of growth is never wasted. As you begin the process of choosing to keep your thoughts and emotions in a high vibration, you will have doubts about the whole idea, and you will feel skeptical. I know you will, because it's a new way of living and thinking. Your ego will feel threatened and will try to stop your progress. What is important is that you keep on practicing. Even if you can only do this for a short time at first, every step you take will help you to grow and move closer to your goal. No movement toward a goal of growing and expanding your life is ever in vain. Sometimes in my life I have thought that I was just too tired to keep this positive vibration going. I have felt worn out. What do I do when I feel this way? I just *feel* the way I feel and take some time to get the rest I need. I know that it's okay to be tired, and it's okay to take some time to fill my own tank, to nurture and care for my soul and my body. You can rest whenever you need to—remember that your life is a journey and that this will be a process.

If you could get only *one* thing from this book, I would hope that you get this: You are *always* creating! Since *all* of your thoughts create, why not put some effort into creating a life you *love* instead of a life of just getting by? Take care to focus on positive thoughts and uplifting feelings. One of the best ways to do this is with gratitude. When you are thankful, you open up a whole new world to yourself. I believe that thanking God may be the *easiest* way to stay in a positive vibration. I am not trying to say that being thankful is easy, because things don't always go the way we *think* they should. I just know that trying to remember a whole list of things to do is harder than remembering *one thing*: thanking God!

So how do you choose to be thankful when life is frequently painful and difficult? I have thought often about this Bible verse: "In everything give thanks; for this is God's will for you in Christ Jesus" (1Thess. 5:18 NAS). I used to think, *What? This circumstance is God's will for me?* For me, that was not the correct interpretation. My perception of this verse is that "this" does not refer to the circumstances you are in, but rather to giving thanks. In other words—this verse says that *giving thanks in all things* is God's will for me. Why would this be God's will when he knows how hard life is sometimes?

Chapter 13 Co-Creating Your Life

All of life is a classroom, and we are always learning. The universe/God does not do things *to* us, but *for* us. Everything that comes into our lives can be used for good: to help us learn about ourselves, to learn more about how to live this life, and how to deal with situations and other people. Anyone can be thankful when things are going great and the blessings are pouring down on us. There is no growth or challenge in that! When the challenges come, we can say, "God, I choose to thank you *in* these circumstances, not *for* these circumstances. I trust that you know the big picture and will work all things for my good." What is good for me? Learning, growing, and evolving as a spiritual being in a human body.

I had quite a struggle the first few years of my insurance career making a living with a straight commission job. I was troubled about it and unhappy. Every day I had to figure out how to make money. In a straight commission job, it can be like starting your job all over again each day. When you are an independent contractor (self-employed), everything depends on what you do.

At some point, I decided to bring my struggle to the universe and began to thank God for a job that I loved. Eventually, everything changed.

I did not get a different and better job. What happened was, I began to *love* the job I *had*. Being thankful doesn't change God—it changes *you*!

"If the only prayer you ever pray in your entire life is thank you, it will be enough."

—Meister Eckhardt

Chapter 14

Visualization

"Imagination is everything. It is the preview of life's coming attractions."

—Albert Einstein

One of the most wonderful things that God gave to you is your imagination. When God created you, He blessed you with this amazing gift. It is one of the most important faculties that you have! I want to share with you how to use your imagination to create the life you love. This chapter will be great fun for me, because I will share my own stories from the last thirty years about how using my imagination has impacted my life!

In reference to my job, you have seen how God changed my heart, and I began to love what I was doing. Here is something I didn't tell you. When I started my insurance job, I began to ask the universe for trips—not just *any* trips, mind you, but *free* trips and fabulous ones at that! I would sit in my glider rocker with some soft instrumental music playing and close my eyes. This is the first step to imagining your future, although you don't need a glider rocker. Then, in my mind's eye, I would envision myself sitting on the most beautiful beach I could imagine. There on the beach, the chair beneath me was so comfortable. The ocean was sparkling, and the seagulls flying overhead were singing. I could hear and see the waves of the ocean rolling in. I could feel a gentle breeze on my face as I sat under a brightly colored umbrella. The sun was shining high overhead and my bare feet were playing in the warm sand. I would put my head back and smile, breathing in the scents, hearing the sounds, and feeling the warmth. I took a bite of a mesquite-barbequed kettle chip and soaked in the flavor (no calories or fat in my imagination). I felt *so* blessed and *so* excited to be sitting on this beautiful beach that all I could do was thank God over and over.

This picture contains everything you need to create the life you love. When you visualize, you need to *see* yourself vividly—doing that which you dream of. You need to *feel* the emotions of your dream *fulfilled*. You need to hear, touch, and taste everything in your imagination—just as if you were there. You need to express gratitude that your dream *has come true* and thank the Universe for bringing you this blessing. I cannot stress this enough. In order to attract what you *want* in your life, you must vividly

Chapter 14 Visualization

picture *every* detail as already accomplished. You must *feel* excited and joyful as you imagine the reality of your dream!

Did I ever get to sit on the beach I imagined? I absolutely did—free flight, free room, free food—everything just as I had imagined. It did not come the day after I imagined it, but it did come. It has come many times in my life. I mean, trips are nice, but free trips are *awesome*! My first free trip was to Phoenix. The next one was a Caribbean cruise and included sitting on a beach with my feet in the sand. The next trip was to Ireland and was amazing! The next trip was to the Bellagio in Las Vegas. The next trip was to Hawaii … you get the picture. I even got to bring my best friend along for free and spend time with other friends while on the trips.

When we went on the Caribbean cruise, the company I worked for bought out the entire Royal Caribbean cruise ship for all of us. The ship was filled with all the qualifiers from all over the United States. Now, I wasn't the highest producer in the company, so the room we had was an inside room with not even a window. I was okay with this, but really wanted more. When we were at sea, someone made the announcement that since there had been some cancellations on this cruise, they were going to give away a few balcony suites that weren't occupied. All you had to do was put your business card into a box and they would draw out the names of the lucky winners. I immediately went to where the box was and put my business card into the drawing. I began to imagine sitting on the balcony of the room, looking out over the beautiful ocean waves, sipping on a Diet Coke, and feeling *so* blessed.

We were sitting visiting with some friends on the deck, when an announcement came over the loudspeakers, "The winners of the balcony suites have been drawn, and you will be notified by phone if you are one of the lucky winners." I immediately got up and said, "I've got to get back to the room because our phone will be ringing." I was certain of it! I opened my door and heard—you guessed it—the phone ringing. I picked it up, and they congratulated me on winning a balcony suite. There were literally thousands of people on this ship and I was one of the few chosen. I wasn't chosen because I was special, I was chosen because I imagined it and thanked God for it *before* it came—and was certain it was coming!

Chapter 14 Visualization

That's just a small thing, you say? Well how about this? One year while still working with insurance, my state manager told me he had a certain production number he wanted our team to achieve for the year.

He said, "Can you guys do it?"

I said, "I believe we can!" So he decided to make a deal with me.

"What do you want if your team reaches this goal?" he said.

"How about a trip to Las Vegas with tickets to see Celine Dion at Caesar's Palace," I replied.

"Okay," he said, "you're on."

Needless to say, I did a lot of visualizing: Celine singing and me *so* enjoying the concert and the surroundings. Not only did we get to fly to Vegas for free and stay for free, but we also had *front row center* seats to see Celine, and she sang right to us. We also received autographed pictures from her.

Still too small, you say? How about this? I really wanted to find a house that I loved, and I wanted to own it. This was very early in my insurance career, before things had really taken off for me. One day I saw, on the edge of town, a house I had never noticed before. The house had a For Sale sign in the front yard, and there was no one living in it. I ran all around the house and looked in the windows. It seemed just perfect for me! I got the phone number from the sign and called the owner of the house. I said I wanted to see it, so we met and she took me on a tour of the house. I loved it! I went to a banker that I had once gotten a small loan from. I had borrowed money to buy some music equipment and had paid him back on time. He was very nice to me, but he politely said he could not give me a loan, as my income was too low. As I told you, I was an independent contractor at the time, and my tax return showed a measly $7,000 of earnings for the previous year. I asked him again nicely if he would reconsider. He said he really couldn't, due to my income. He was the bank president and the buck stopped with him—literally.

    This is what I did next: I went to the house I was currently living in and sat in my chair and began to visualize myself driving up to the garage door of the home I wanted to buy. I would hit the garage door opener, see the door come open, and drive into the garage. I saw myself smiling and *feeling so happy* as I walked into my new home. It was furnished with all of my furniture. I would

Chapter 14 Visualization

look around and rejoice at how much I loved my place. I was so thankful that it was mine, and I thanked God for it. I did this every day for a couple of weeks. Then I called the banker and asked him *again* if he would reconsider and give me the loan. He said that he would really like to, but couldn't, due to my income.

I continued to imagine myself driving into the garage and coming into the house, so blessed to *own* and *live* in the home I really wanted to buy, seeing my furniture there, and loving its coziness. I did this for a few more weeks and then I decided to talk with the banker again—and ask for the fourth time! I drove to the bank, which was in a nearby town and politely asked him again. He said to me, "You know, I shouldn't really do this, but because you have been so persistent and I know your character, I will give you the loan." I was thrilled, but not surprised, because I *believed* that the house would be mine and the universe would bring it to pass.

Can you see how imagination plays such an important part in bringing our dreams to pass? Your imagination is more powerful than you know! It is *always* working, even when you are not intentionally imagining what you want. If you are imagining all the bad things that could happen to you, because you are afraid—that works too. You will attract many of the things you do *not* want to happen, because you are imagining your worst fears coming to pass. Whenever you have a thought, you also have a picture in your head. If I mention a snow-capped mountain, instantly in your mind you see a snow-capped mountain. Your mind works with pictures and "sees" what you think about. You do have a choice in what you imagine. Why not choose something intentionally that you will be blessed by? Living with joy and thankfulness because you have imagined all the wonderful good that is in your life is actually fun! You can choose to do this anytime you want to. It may take some time to accomplish your dream. As you saw earlier, I won that national singing contest after four years of competing. For *four years* I imagined myself singing on that stage, feeling excited, blessed, and seeing myself signing autographs after I was awarded the top prize!

Visualization is often used as a mental rehearsal technique in sports. It is a very powerful tool and many studies have been done to test this. You may have heard of Dr. Judd Blaslotto at the University of Chicago who conducted a well-known study. He split people into three groups and tested each group on how many free throws

Chapter 14 Visualization

they could make. After this, he had the first group practice free throws every day for an hour. The second group just visualized themselves making free throws. The third group did nothing. After thirty days, he tested them again. The first group improved by 24 percent. The second group improved by 23 percent without touching a basketball! The third group did not improve, which was expected.

When I began to really understand how this principle of visualization worked, it changed my whole life—and it changed my prayer life. When I pray for someone now, I always choose to see the person in my imagination as smiling and happy and in good health. I see them and I hear them say to me how they are encouraged, they are happy, and they are blessed. If they are struggling with an illness or other problem, I see them as healthy and happy. I do not beg and plead with God to bless those that I love—I see them in my imagination being blessed and prospered! As you can see, I use this method not just in praying for my own life, but for others as well.

A few years ago, my youngest son, Justin, who is a singer/songwriter, was traveling with a band and singing all over the United States. He told me he was lonely and wanted to find someone to love. It is very difficult to meet someone when you are always on the road. I began to visualize him coming through the door of my house holding hands with a beautiful, blond young lady. They were both smiling and happy and so excited about life! I did this day after day—it was my prayer for him. After a while, a young lady he had admired from afar in college saw him on Facebook and messaged him. He was so excited because he remembered who she was and had wanted to date her. He had not asked her out because back then she was dating a friend of his. He was living in Minneapolis when he wasn't on the road, and she was living near Denver. In his travels, he found himself in Colorado. He called her and asked her to meet him for a coffee. Let me share with you a few lyrics from a song he wrote and recorded describing this encounter.

> I can't believe it—it's snowing again up in this pass.
>
> It's like the heavens screaming out to me, "aw, come on ... take her hand."
>
> But we just met, so we head downtown like the rest to grab a drink,

Chapter 14 Visualization

But I'm thinking 'bout where I'm gonna buy the ring.

I wanna fall into your arms.

I wanna let this evening go.

I wanna wake up with your arm around my side.

After all, that's all I really want—from now on, she's all I really want.

I love this song, and I am having trouble writing this, because my eyes are filled with tears of happiness. At this writing, they have been married for four years and love each other dearly. She is blond, by the way—just like my visualization.

I will share with you one more of my prayers involving my kids. My oldest son, Jacob, and his wife had a son (my first grandchild) seven years ago. They named him Justin. Before little Justin was born, they had a miscarriage. A couple of years after they had Justin, they had another miscarriage. They really wanted more children and were told by a doctor that the chances of them ever having another baby were 0.5 percent. This was very difficult for them to hear, and they really prayed that God would give them another child. I also prayed, and my prayer was a *visualization* of them coming through the door to my house with my young grandson, Justin. In my imagination, I saw my daughter-in-law carrying a baby, and Justin was excited, saying, "Grandma Vicki, this is my new baby brother!" In my picture, my son, his wife, and my grandson were all smiling and full of joy—they were just beaming. Today, Justin is the big brother to not one but *two* healthy little brothers! Again, tears of joy are flowing as I write this.

On a light and fun note, here is another example of my prayer/visualizations being fulfilled. I had been *visualizing* for several weeks that there were stacks of money (bills banded together in a bundle) sitting on my kitchen table. Every time I would see them in my imagination, I would feel all tingly and happy to be the owner of all these bundles of cash! I just knew that one day they would be sitting on my kitchen table.

I had a business trip scheduled, so I headed to the territory conference, where there were hundreds of people gathered. At this conference there were several prizes given away, and we all put our business cards into a drawing and hoped to win something. The chances of winning anything were slim, because there were so many people gathered there. As you are probably expecting, I *did* get my name called, and I won something. I went to pick up what I had won and saw a little wooden chest that looked just like a treasure chest. When I opened it up, it was full of one-dollar bills banded together in several bundles. There in that treasure chest was $1,400! It was such synchronicity—that the money was in several bundles, banded together, just like my visualization. When I got home, I took out all the bundles of money from the chest, laid them on my kitchen table, and just looked at the vision before me—the vision that had become a reality.

I bring up this example to point out that when you put an intention out into the universe and visualize it, you need to be very specific about all the details. The more specific you are about what you are seeking, the better. Remember, your subconscious mind does not know the difference between reality and imagination. Whatever you plant, it will bring forth through the energy of your thoughts, emotions, and visualizations. This is how the laws of our universe work!

The number of experiences that God has brought to me through my prayers/visualizations is astounding—I could go on and on. I have a notebook that I have kept from 1989 all the way to 2013. I had written my prayer requests in this notebook and documented how they were answered. Not everything I visualized became a reality, but many things did! As I said earlier, sometimes during the course of my life my desires and my dreams changed, and so I changed what I was praying for. Sometimes, looking back, I can see how what I thought I wanted then would not have been the best for me. I suppose I would call this my spiritual evolution.

I want to share one more story with you. This is a story of two people I know who worked *together* with God to co-create their lives. Both of them had been divorced, living single and alone for a number of years. Eventually, they both became lonely and had a longing for someone to share their lives with. One of them started looking into online dating sites. She began the process of trying to find someone and continued for several weeks, just searching. She also took time each day to *visualize* meeting that one person who would be special to her, who would be kind and honest and loving. In her imagination, she would see them together talking and laughing, feeling happy and excited about sharing the rest of their lives together. She would do this day after day.

Chapter 14 Visualization

    The other person had no computer, but suddenly decided to go out and buy one to look into online dating sights. *Three days* after firing up the new computer and going online, the two of them met at a dating site. They began to talk online and then began to talk on the phone. Six weeks later they met in person. They each *knew* that they had found their life partner, so they kept seeing each other for a whole year—trying to spend as much time together as they could. You see, they didn't live in close proximity, and it took a while to work out the details of being able to move, sell a home, find a job, and put everything in order so that they could make a commitment to each other. Actually, they were from *different countries*! To make a long story short, this couple has been together and committed to each other now for over fourteen years. They are very happy and live in a small town in rural Minnesota. I know this is a true story because one of them is *me*!

    When you ponder this, do you think it was just coincidence? My partner and I have *no* doubts that the power of prayer and the grace of God brought us together. We certainly couldn't have done it by ourselves!

The truth is, we all have a "tool chest" full of tools to work with while we are on earth. We have our thoughts, our emotions, our imaginations, our will, the ability to choose, and our desire. We all have the same *tools,* but we don't all know how to use those tools to build a life we love. Sometimes we use them to inadvertently build a life that doesn't serve us well. The thing is we all need to learn about *how* to use these tools to build a better life. My hope is that as you progress through this book, you are gaining some insight and expanding your awareness of your own gifts and how to use the tools that God has given you.

"Abundance exists all around us—in nature, in our local grocery stores, in the deep love of our friends and families—everywhere in the universe. ... If I experience lack of any kind, I may be thinking there is a limited supply available to me. Although the abundance of God's good is as vast as the ocean, I can only carry as much water as my container will hold. If I want to enjoy more, I must enlarge my container—expand my consciousness."

—Deepak Chopra

Chapter 15
What If Your Dreams Are Not Becoming Reality

"It's not what you are that holds you back; it's what you think you are not."

—Denis Waitley

What if you started to practice some of the strategies that I have spoken about in this book and it doesn't seem to be working for you? Well, there could be many reasons. One might be that you haven't been using these strategies for very long. As you have seen from my experience, some of the dreams that we have do take longer to materialize than others. The key to this issue is *patience*.

Also, it could be that you are new at visualizing and you are just learning how to do it. When I started, it took a little while for me to be able to really *see* pictures in my imagination the way I wanted to. I learned that it was kind of like watching a movie in my mind. There needed to be movement and color and sound in my imaginings, just as there are in a movie theater. When we are in a theater we vividly see everything up on that screen. We see all the colors and the movement. We also hear the sounds vividly as well. It took a while for me to actually *see* myself in the picture, *hear* myself, and *feel* the emotions that were so crucial to creating a better life. Emotions like joy, thankfulness, and excitement are keys to creating. This all takes practice! It will not happen overnight, so please give it some time.

It might also be that you are dealing with the same thing we all have. Everyone has a set point in his or her self-image. The best example I have found to describe this is a thermostat. You know that when you set a thermostat at a certain temperature it will always keep your home at the same temperature. It will not go above or below the temperature that you have set it to. Our self-image is like a thermostat in that we all have some limiting beliefs about ourselves. Some of these beliefs we chose ourselves as we were growing up. We also have limiting beliefs that have been downloaded into our subconscious by others when we were children, and we have adopted their beliefs as our own. These are beliefs that we are *not aware of*, because they are below our level of conscious thinking. As I said earlier, our subconscious mind is much more powerful than

Chapter 15 *What If Your Dreams Are Not Becoming Reality?*

our conscious mind and is often running our lives without our knowledge. If our subconscious mind does not agree with what our conscious mind is saying there will be no change. If you try to push past your set point with thoughts, feelings, and visualizations about how you deserve success and happiness, it won't work if the subconscious is saying, "I don't deserve to be happy. I am not bright enough to be successful," and so on. This is the self-sabotage of the subconscious mind.

So if you wanted to earn $100,000 per year and your subconscious is saying, "I can never earn six figures," your thermostat will always keep you set below six figures. Even if you earned $100,000 one year, you probably wouldn't be able to sustain that kind of income if your self-image is telling you that you can't.

Another possibility is that you have an emotional block that is inhibiting your growth. Our feelings are meant to come up and flow through us as we experience life. If something that I perceive as hurtful happens to me but I don't allow myself to feel sad and talk about my feelings, those feelings can become blocked within me. They did not flow *through* me but were trapped *inside* of me. We all have some emotional blocks that need clearing. We have blocks regarding experiences that we did not complete. For example, we were hurt by what someone said to us, but did not process those emotions by *feeling* them and then *talking* about them. Or perhaps we were hurt by what someone did to us but did not work through those emotions. Because we did not express our feelings about the experience, we would have the remnants of that experience stored within as a painful feeling or memory (also referred to as a block). We have blocks around our *own* judgment of our feelings and our lack of acceptance of who we are.

Sometimes we don't forgive ourselves for things that we believe we should not have done. Cheryl Richardson is a best-selling author, speaker, and personal coach. She puts it like this, "What locks our fear in place, our anxiety in place, our inability to take action, our inability to achieve the kind of life we want to achieve, is a lack of self-acceptance and a lack of self-forgiveness. Resistance to accept ourselves as we are keeps us stuck."

What can you do about this? You need to work to change your limiting beliefs about yourself and, therefore, your self-image. There are many strategies that can help you. The one that I most prefer is called Emotional Freedom Technique, or EFT. I first learned about this

Chapter 15 What If Your Dreams Are Not Becoming Reality?

technique by watching a documentary film called *The Tapping Solution* by Nick Ortner. I have since read Nick's book by the same title and have seen firsthand how this technique can benefit our lives. Here is how Nick describes this powerful strategy:

> Tapping, also known as EFT, is a powerful tool for improving your life on multiple levels: mental, emotional, and physical. Based on the principles of both ancient acupressure and modern psychology, tapping concentrates on specific meridian endpoints, while focusing on negative emotions or physical sensations. Combined with spoken word, tapping helps calm the nervous system to restore the balance of the energy in the body and rewire the brain to respond in healthy ways.

Several studies have been done that document how successful tapping is for many kinds of disorders and issues. Currently, tapping is being used by many different kinds of practitioners in the healthcare field. The unique thing about tapping is that you can use it yourself—you do not need to see a doctor or psychologist to implement this remarkable strategy. For more information on tapping, I would recommend that you check out Nick Ortner's website for more details: www.tappingsolution.com. You might also want to pick up his book, as it is easy to understand and contains helpful scripts that you can use to promote your own personal health.

As we talk about the energy system within our bodies, I would like to remind you that as humans we *are* energy, and we have a vibration that is emitted from us at all times, even though we are not aware of it. If our energy system isn't functioning well, our vibrational frequency is lowered. This can cause other problems within us such as fear and depression.

Qigong (pronounced *chee-gong*) is another powerful tool that can be used to help heal this energy flow problem. "Qi" means life-energy and "gong" means work or exercise. This exercise has been practiced in China for thousands of years. Studies have shown that Qigong has many positive effects on health and well being. When I feel an abundance of stress in my life I use this practice and find it to have a very calming and centering effect. If you would like to get more information on Qigong, you could visit this website: www.modernqigong.com, which is Lee Holden's site. Lee was featured on a PBS special and has quite a story of healing himself.

Chapter 15 What If Your Dreams Are Not Becoming Reality?

I have also used and enjoyed meditations from this site: www.mindbodytraining.com. I know that you can search "meditation" and find many online sites that would be helpful.

Anything you want to do well, you need to practice. If you want to live your life well—to grow, to open up, to give to yourself and to the world—you will need to practice. If you want to raise your level of consciousness and your energy level, you will need to practice. If you really desire to create a life you love, you will need to practice. You don't need to be perfect; this is a process, and as you grow, you will need to keep practicing. If you want to live an extraordinary life, you can't just coast. If you want to coast, then by all means do, but if you want *more* and want to create and contribute, you will need to practice. Don't be so afraid of failing that you don't try. You won't get everything right the first time. No one ever does. This path you are on will become easier as you travel it. It will become more exciting and more fulfilling too. This journey *is* the destination of your life!

"Life should not be a journey to the grave with the intention of arriving safely in a pretty and well-preserved body, but rather to skid in broadside in a cloud of smoke, thoroughly used up, totally worn out, and loudly proclaiming Wow! What a ride!"

—Hunter S. Thompson

Chapter 16

It's All About Love

"So in everything, do to others what you would have them do to you, for this sums up the Law and the Prophets."

—Matt. 7:12 NIV

The above verse is one we all know and is referred to as the Golden Rule. I grew up with this verse and everyone telling me how I should treat others the way I wanted to be treated—in other words, to be nice. That made sense to me. However, there are really two reasons you would want to be kind to others. The first reason is because it is the *right thing to do.* The second reason is because it is a law of the universe that if you are kind to others, you will receive kindness yourself. If you are helpful to others you will also receive helpfulness from others in your own life. If you give financially to help others, you will receive financial rewards as well. It may not be immediately, but it will come if you are faithful in giving. This is God's law. So the deeper meaning isn't just to be nice. The point is that if you are good to other people, God will also be good to you. What a sweet deal!

Here is another verse that I think is key, "You shall love your neighbor as yourself" (Mark 12:31 RSV). What I see implied here is that if you do *not* love yourself, you will also *not* love your neighbor. If you think that you love yourself but you are not kind to others—think again. It all starts with *you loving yourself.* We can only give what we *have*. If you give more love and acceptance to yourself, you will have more love and acceptance to give to others. If you are forgiving and kind with yourself, you can also be that way with others. If you are understanding and gentle with yourself, you will be able to be understanding and gentle with others. In like manner, if you are critical and judgmental of yourself, you will most likely be that way with others. If you are harsh and unforgiving with yourself, that will also show up as you relate to others. You are loved by God, and you deserve to be treated with respect and kindness. You deserve this as much as any other child of God. This is not selfishness—this is the birthright given to you by your Creator. If you can give this to *yourself,* you will become a light in this world.

As Brennan Manning has written, "Never confuse your *perception* of yourself with the mystery that you really *are* accepted." He also said, "The outstretched arms of Jesus exclude no one, neither the drunk in the doorway, the

Chapter 16 *It's All About Love*

panhandler on the street, gays and lesbians in their isolation, the most selfish and ungrateful in their cocoons, the most unjust of employers, and the most overweening of snobs. The love of Christ embraces all without exception." Since the love of Christ embraces all, we would do well to remember this as it relates to ourselves.

These words by Henri Nouwen have greatly impacted my life:

> Our preciousness, uniqueness, and individuality are not given to us by those who meet us in clock-time—our brief chronological existence—but by the One who has chosen us with an everlasting love, a love that existed from all eternity and will last through all eternity. ... The truth ... is that I am the chosen child of God, precious in God's eyes, called the Beloved from all eternity and held safe in an everlasting embrace. ... Instead of making us feel that we are better, more precious or valuable than others, our awareness of being chosen opens our eyes to the chosenness of others. That is the great joy of being chosen: the discovery that others are chosen as well ... once we deeply trust that we ourselves are precious in God's eyes, we are able to

recognize the preciousness of others and their unique places in God's heart.

As you think about your relationship to God and to others in this world, give some thought as to how you could make a positive difference in someone's life today. This day is all you have. This day is all I have. None of us knows what will happen tomorrow, and yesterday is gone. *Now* is the time to love yourself and *now* is the time to reach out to others and share your unique light with the world. Ultimately, we all live in the *now*. We cannot live in the future. We can think about and plan for the future, but when we get there, it will be our *now*. The right time to give love is always now. Here and now you can make a difference!

In the words of Wendy Mass, "Be kind always, for everyone you meet is fighting a battle you know nothing about."

I have found this to be true. We are all living life, and this life is often filled with challenges and difficulties. One word of encouragement from someone can brighten your day, and one act of kindness from you can be uplifting to another.

Chapter 16 It's All About Love

Mother Theresa said, "In this life we cannot always do great things, but we can do small things with great love."

Dr. Lissa Rankin stresses how love and gratitude are the glue that holds everything together. Let me share with you a true story I heard her tell about a man from Greece. His name was Stamatis Moraitis. He immigrated to the US and settled in Florida where he met his wife. She was Greek-American, and together they had three children. As he moved into his sixties, he went to see a doctor because he was experiencing some shortness of breath. The doctor told him that he had cancer, and he had only nine months to live. Because he wasn't pleased with what that doctor said, he went to eight more doctors for their opinions. They all told him the same thing—his cancer was incurable, and he had only nine months to live.

Stamatis and his wife decided to move back to where he had grown up—the Greek island of Ikaria. When they moved in with his parents, he was not feeling well. Soon people heard that he was home and they started visiting him. Several friends and family members came often, bringing with them food, wine, and games. They spent much time together sharing laughter, drinking wine, and playing games. Six months went by, and Stamatis seemed to be feeling better. He even planted a garden and the family started eating what he had grown. He began to tend grapes and make some wine. He started going back to his church, walking there each week. Presently, Stamatis is cancer free—and ninety-eight years old.

There is a very interesting ending to this story. Long after Stamatis was first diagnosed, he went back to the United States to see all of the doctors who had told him he had nine months to live. Strangely enough, all nine doctors were dead.

Love, gratitude, the fellowship of friends and family, a life with purpose, productive work, exercise, and healthy food all contributed to this gentleman's ability to live a long and happy life. We can all learn a great deal from his story.

If you take care of yourself, invest time in yourself, find something that you love to do, and do it—then you are taking steps toward fulfilling your purpose here on earth. If you use each day to tend to your own needs, and then to give to others in need, you are on the right path.

Chapter 16 It's All About Love

"Jesus said the world is going to recognize you as His by only one sign: the way you are with one another on the street every day. You are going to leave people feeling a little better or a little worse. You're going to affirm them or deprive them, but there'll be no neutral exchange."

—Brennan Manning

In Closing

"You are always one choice away from changing your life. One choice, just one, can change your life forever. Simply put, your life today is what your choices have made it, but with new choices, you can change directions this very moment."

—Mac Anderson

Here is my last question to you: Do you deserve to be rich? Do you deserve to have riches in your friendships, in your family relationships, in your spiritual connection with the infinite? Do you deserve an abundant life—abundant in love, in health, in success, in joy, in hope, in peace, in money?

The answer is *yes*, and the reason that you are deserving is because of *one thing*—you are a child of God. I'm just a girl from a small town in Iowa. Growing up I never believed that I was deserving—but *I am*, and *you are too*, because we are both children of the one power in all the universe, our God. Our Father loves us as much as he loves his son, Jesus. One of my favorite verses is: "Do not be afraid, little flock, for your Father has chosen gladly to give you the kingdom" (Luke 12:32 NAS). As I shared

In Closing

earlier, Jesus said that he came so that we might be able to live life abundantly. That means not just someday in a future heaven, but *now, here*—on earth!

I want you to know that you can live a life you *love*! The kinds of wonderful things that I have been blessed with can bless you too. I am blessed not because I am more special than you, not because I am more talented, or more unique. You are equally unique and talented. I have been blessed because I changed my thinking and my energy. I chose to change and become open and receptive to the abundance that is all around us in this world. There is enough abundance for everyone, and you can claim yours too!

Remember, as we talk about dreams—whatever dream you are longing for is worthwhile. If your dream will bless your life and be a blessing to others, it is important. Maybe your dream is to forgive someone who hurt you, to love and cherish your family more, to become physically healthy and fit, to lose weight, to be kinder to others, to give more money and time to those in need—whatever it is, it is important, because it is important to you.

Make a decision about what you are going to bring into your life. Choose to take some quiet time each day to connect with your source. You may not think you have the time, but we all have the same twenty-four hours each day. Whatever you spend your time on, *that* is what is important to you. It's your choice.

If you choose to spend ten to fifteen minutes each day for just twenty-one days on your own personal growth and development, you will be on track to creating a life you love. Write your dream down. Spend time *in* your dream, visualize in your imagination, and see your dream as *already accomplished.* See yourself feeling joyful and so thankful to God that your dream is fulfilled. See yourself giving love and kindness to others around you. Also act on your dream: Whatever small or big thing you can do to help bring your dream about—do *it.*

God's promises aren't for certain "special" people—they are for everyone. If you are breathing, you are eligible! The world is waiting for your vision, and no one can bring your vision to the world but you. As George Eliot said, "It is never too late to be what you might have been."

Practice each day keeping your thoughts thankful. I cannot over-stress how important this is! These words from Martha Smock have had a huge influence on me:

In Closing

Do not wait to give thanks until every prayer is answered. Do not wait to give thanks until things are perfect. Give thanks where you are, in the present set of circumstances, in the conditions in which you find yourself. Give thanks for life; give thanks for this day at hand. Give thanks for the opportunities to grow and learn. Your attitude of thankfulness lifts you out of any feeling of depression, out of any feeling of loneliness. Give thanks to God and look at life with a thankful spirit. (excerpt from Listen, Beloved)

While writing this book, I realized that I had done years of life coaching in my management positions at work and in my personal life as well. Because of that, I decided to become certified—as a life coach. If you are reading this, then you know that I pursued another one of my dreams, and I am now a certified life coach. Thank you, God! Only a bucket of dreams left to go.

"Twenty years from now you will be more disappointed by the things that you didn't do than by the ones you did do. So throw off the bowlines. Sail away from the safe harbor. Catch the trade winds in your sails. Explore. Dream. Discover."

—Mark Twain

Dear Reader,

Thank you so much for taking this journey with me. If you liked this book and gained insight into your own journey—read it again!

If you didn't understand or appreciate the concepts presented here—put this book on a shelf, and pull it out again in a few months or next year. You are growing and evolving. Perhaps in the future this book will make a difference in your life.

Blessings,

Vicki Lynn

About the Author

Vicki Lynn King is a certified life coach, as well as an award-winning singer/songwriter. She is also an author and motivational speaker. Vicki has been touching people's lives through her speaking and singing for over thirty years.

She was educated as a registered nurse and spent several years helping others in the healthcare field. She then expanded her vision and moved into the corporate world of insurance, becoming a team leader and regional manager for a Fortune 200 company. In working as a team builder in the corporate world, she coached her associates on how to succeed in business and life. Vicki continues to coach and teach others how to move past their current life circumstances, find their life purpose, and build a life they love.

Author's Website: www.vickilynking.com

If you would like a copy of Vicki's latest music CD, please visit www.cdbaby.com/cd/vickilynnking. There you can listen to, order, or download her album.

If you would like to connect with Vicki on Facebook, visit

www.facebook.com/vickilynnking1

For information on her life coaching please visit

www.vickilynnking.lifemasteryinstitute.com/

Notes

Made in the USA
Charleston, SC
18 May 2015